HOPE

One Man's Journey of Discovery
from Tormented Child
to Social Worker
to Spiritual Director

MARSHALL JUNG

HOPE
One Man's Journey of Discovery from Tormented Child
to Social Worker to Spiritual Director
by Marshall Jung

Edited by Michael Coyne
Design and typesetting by Patricia A. Lynch

Copyright © 2015 by Marshall Jung

Published by In Extenso Press
Distributed exclusively by ACTA Publications, 4848 N. Clark Street, Chicago, IL 60640, (800) 397-2282, www.actapublications.com

Scripture quotations are from the *New Revised Standard Version Bible*, copyright © 1989 by the Division of Christian Education of the National Council of the Churches of Christ in the USA. Used by permission.

Emily Dickinson poem on page 7 is from *The Poems of Emily Dickinson*, edited by Thomas H. Johnson, Cambridge, Mass.: The Belknap Press of Harvard University Press, Copyright © 1951, 1955, 1979, 1983 by the President and Fellows of Harvard College.

All rights reserved. No part of this publication may be reproduced or transmitted in any form or by any means, electronic, digital, or mechanical, including photocopying and recording, or by any information storage and retrieval system, including the Internet, without permission from the publisher. Permission is hereby given to use short excerpts with proper citation in reviews and marketing copy, newsletters, bulletins, class handouts, and scholarly papers.

Library of Congress Catalog Number: 2015932393
ISBN: 978-0-87946-990-0
Printed in the United States of America by Total Printing Systems
Year 25 24 23 22 21 20 19 18 17 16 15
Printing 12 11 10 9 8 7 6 5 4 3 2 First

✪ Text printed on 30% post-consumer recycled paper

Contents

Message to Readers 5

Introduction 7

Chapter 1
Bathed in Warmth and Love 21

Chapter 2
Time of Loneliness and the Emergence of Shame 25

Chapter 3
Hope and Disillusionment 41

Chapter 4
Immersion in Guilt and Despair 49

Chapter 5
My Vocation Finds Me 61

Chapter 6
Gift of Freedom 91

Chapter 7
Transformation from Religiosity to Spirituality 107

Chapter 8
Evolution into a Spiritually Based Practitioner 125

Chapter 9
Caring for Souls 149

Epilogue 167

Notes 169

Resources 170

Acknowledgments 171

This book is dedicated to Rosie,
my *anam cara*.

Message to the Reader

 I am a seventy-year-old, Chinese American, Roman Catholic man, married for fifty years, who has taken many paths during my travels throughout life. One of those paths has been a forty-three year career in social work. In this profession I have served in the capacity of community organizer, agency executive, professor, trainer, supervisor, consultant, clinician, and spiritual director. I have provided services to numerous racial and ethnic groups. I have also served, either directly or indirectly, those faced with poverty and lack of upward mobility; those suffering from institutional racism and discrimination based on gender, sexual orientation, and ethnicity; those carrying the emotional scars from being sexually and physically abused, neglected and exploited; those seeking peace in their disability, illness, and dying; those suffering from a crisis or lost in the abyss of a trauma; those searching for meaning in the midst of a natural or manmade disaster; those imprisoned in the darkness of their mental illness; those seeking reconciliation in their unfulfilling marriages; and those drowning in their feelings of worthlessness, alienation, and loneliness.

In short, my life's work, my vocation, has been dedicated to using my talents and skills to serve the underprivileged, underserved, and those most in need of social, emotional, and spiritual comfort and support. Several years ago I discovered that at the heart of my profession and work is compassion and that our primary mission, no matter what our specialty, is to offer loving kindness and hope to those we serve.

My purpose in this book is to share with you from a Catholic and personal perspective how God uses hope to influence, shape, direct, enrich, and—most importantly—transform our life from one that focuses upon the cares of the world to one that is interiorly directed and concerned about living a spiritually enriching existence. In this light I wish to convey that because of God's infinite love, the Holy Spirit is always—especially in the midst of our darkest hours, greatest despair, and deepest feelings of alienation, confusion, and loneliness—reaching out and offering us hope. The narrative through which I will be conveying my understanding regarding this supernatural virtue will be through the sharing of my story, the lessons I learned from it, and how I was unknowingly led to serving God by first becoming a therapist, and later a spiritually based practitioner and spiritual director. It will also be conveyed through the lessons I learned from the stories of those whom I have had the privilege to serve. Because every person's story is sacred and needs to be honored, I will not, unless given permission to do so, use any individual's real name. In addition I will use various means, including the use of composites, to protect people's privacy and identity.

Although I will be speaking with a Catholic voice, I do not believe Catholicism or Christianity is the only path to God, the Divine, or living a spiritual life. I believe God has many voices. My Christian voice, for example, has been greatly influenced by the voices of Confucianism, Taoism, Zen Buddhism, Sufism, Jewish mysticism, and Native American spirituality. In fact, I do not believe having faith in any organized religion or philosophy is a prerequisite to living in hope and having access to the Divine Presence. These beliefs don't really stray far away from the Catholic Church's doctrine. Without denying its teaching regarding its primacy, the church acknowledges that God's grace is available to those of other traditions and even to non-believers. I believe God, who by definition is omnipotent, will find a way to speak with everyone regardless of whether or not we recognize the Divine Presence. Finally, I will be using the masculine pronoun in mentioning God, but don't believe that God has a gender and that God is in reality indescribable.

Introduction

"Hope" is the thing with feathers –
That perches in the soul –
And sings the tune without the words –
And never stops – at all –

And sweetest – in the Gale – is heard –
And sore must be the storm –
That could abash the little Bird
That kept so many warm –

I've heard it in the chillest land –
And on the strangest Sea –
Yet, never, in Extremity,
It asked a crumb – of Me.[1]

EMILY DICKINSON

The Transformative Power of Living in Hope

During my travels in life I have come to learn a great deal about the psychology and spirituality of hope. Among many other things, I have learned that hope, like love, is a life force that psychologically gives meaning to our lives and spiritually gives meaning to our existence. I have come to see how hope dances in our hearts and souls, in our consciousness and unconsciousness, and in our friendships and vocations. In addition, I have discovered that it is experienced in the ordinary and the extraordinary, in the observance of butterflies or our grandchildren, and in the sharing of our thoughts and feelings with those we love.

Furthermore, I have experienced on countless occasions the offerings of hope by friends, family members, and service providers to those suffering from various afflictions. I have experienced, as well, how hope resides in courage, inspiration, celebration, and prayer. As a consequence of what I have learned I have come to believe that hope is always present. It is in us and around us, even in our dreams, daily conversations, and cultural icons. And because of what I have learned, I now believe, above all, that hope is *life*, life that knows it is alive; life that celebrates life; life that yearns to be fulfilled in the fullness of truth, intimacy, and love; life in which we intuitively know that the possibilities for psychological, emotional, and spiritual enrichment are as countless as the stars in the sky overhead.

In this book, I have chosen to share with you my insights through the narration of my story because it is through reviewing my own life history that I have come to understand how hope—informed by faith and love—has influenced, directed, and transformed my life. Moreover, while my story, like everyone's story, is sacred and unique, it is really a universal story. It contains themes and issues that each of us has to address as we make our way through life's journey. We all encounter desolation and consolation, suffering and healing, sadness and joy, pain and pleasure, disappointment and happiness, indifference and intimacy. I certainly did. My journey has taught me that if we are to live fully in the beauty and richness that life offers we must meet, challenge, and overcome impediments.

As you will read in the pages ahead, the major challenges in my life were:

- Overcoming my psychological insecurities and sense of shame
- Feelings of loneliness, despair, and hopelessness
- Being unloved by my mother
- Losing my voice
- Struggling about my relationship with my wife Rosie
- The rigidity of the Catholic Church
- My fear of God and damnation

John Donne wrote, "No man is an island" and I must agree. I certainly couldn't have successfully met these challenges on my own. I couldn't have met them without the love and devotion of Rosie, the understanding of my children Richard and Eileen, the compassion and care of endearing friends and colleagues, the support and direction of wonderful teachers and mentors, and without the blessings, love, and intercessions of the Holy Spirit.

As I reflect on my story, I am reminded of Motel the tailor in the musical *Fiddler on the Roof*. Motel was in love with Tzeitl, but in the period in which the story takes place marriages were arranged by parents. Unbeknown to Tzeitl, her father, Tevye, had arranged a marriage for her with Lazer Wolf, the village butcher. Upon learning of the arrangement, Tzeitl immediately ran in desperation to tell her father that she was in love with and wished to marry Motel. But Tevye was startled by this revelation. In Jewish cultural tradition of the time, the idea of children selecting whom they wish to marry was not only beyond comprehension, it was unacceptable. Yet, upon learning of the marriage arrangements that were unfolding, Motel, a very shy, timid, and unassuming young man somehow found the courage, a dormant courage waiting to be discovered, to challenge Tevye, a man of whom he was terrified. Surprising even himself, Motel assertively asked Tevye for Tzeitl's hand in marriage and, breaking with tradition, the old-fashioned father agreed to the request. In that moment, Motel felt a miracle had happened. Celebrating and dancing ecstatically in a nearby meadow with his future bride, a joyful young Motel sang: "...out of a worthless lump of clay, God has made a man today."

Likewise in my life, I feel that God took me, this worthless lump of clay, this lonely, insecure, insignificant, self-deprecating, and unlovable little boy and performed a miracle by transforming him into a man, a man who could live in all the goodness and richness that this world has to offer. For Motel, the vehicle through which God orchestrated his miracle was a woman, his beloved Tzeitl. For me that miracle was Rosie. Because of that woman and our relationship, I came to know the meaning of the phrase, *"Through the power of the Holy Spirit all things can be made new."* I also now know what it feels like to be bathed in faith, hope, and God's infinite love.

Although I now rest in that love, the journey that led me to where I am today was long and difficult. It was, however, a transforming experience, with the transformation expressing itself in three realms. In the realm of faith, it was a transformation from religiosity to spirituality. In the realm of psychology, it was a transformation from psychological insecurity to joyful freedom. And in the realm of work and contribution to society, it was a transformation from being a therapist to being a spiritual guide. In this book, I will be sharing my story through these transformational processes.

The three realms of my life that I just mentioned are not, of course, independent or separate entities; rather they are completely interrelated with each dimension influencing and being influenced by the other. They are like the different ingredients that go into baking and making of a lovely three-tier wedding cake. Mixed, blended, and folded together, the cake's ingredients give it texture, moisture, shape, various flavors, and unique character; they allow it to grow. Meanwhile, the ingredients that are combined for the frosting add to the overall flavor, shape, and beauty. The cake's design gives the appearance that there are three separate cakes, but in reality it is one, with all parts containing the same elements, all elements contributing to the final product's overall character, essence, and integrity.

And so it is with the three dimensions of my life. The elements contained in them mixed, blended, and folded together constitute the one person that is me.

In addition to sharing my story with you, I have chosen to share as well what I have learned about hope through the stories and experiences of others—the people I have worked with as a therapist and spiritual guide. I am doing this because early in my career I discovered that the work I do with others is reciprocal. I am always influenced and transformed by the life stories others share with me. One of the reasons I find my vocation so rewarding is because every client or directee has been my teacher, each teaching me about the beauty that is inherent in everyone—teaching me about honor, courage, fidelity, commitment, love, spirituality, and how the Divine Presence works in our lives. And as a result of what I have learned from others who have shared their deepest life experiences with me, I feel I am now in an informed position to write this book.

The Complexities of Spiritual Journeys

What do I mean when I write about the spiritual journey? The experience to which I am referring is a transformational process that involves both an inward and an outward process, one that has an interconnecting and reciprocal relationship between both dynamics. Foremost, it is an inward journey into ourselves; a journey of reflection, examination, and discernment. It is a journey into self-awareness, affirmation, and wisdom. It is a journey into adventure, discovery, and hope. It is also a journey into reclamation, that is, a reclaiming and embracing of personal and spiritual attributes that have been lost or hidden, attributes that allow us to live more fully in our true self. *Most importantly, it is a journey towards cultivating an intimate relationship with God and into the discovery of the Divine Presence that dwells within us.* Ultimately, these internal discoveries inform and become the major guiding forces that guide our external journey.

The elements that contribute to our external journey include how we psychologically, philosophically, and theologically perceive the world and universe in which we live. They also include the judgments and decisions we make regarding our future and how we conduct our lives in relationship to ourselves, others, our local and world community, and our natural environment.

The spiritual journey is a dynamic and organic process that is forever changing, growing, and being reshaped. Like the blended interplay of a violin and piano in a duet, spiritually our external realities inform and blend with our interior realities, thus allowing us to live in harmony with ourselves, others, and the world.

A central message of this book is that I believe we are all on—or should be on—a spiritual journey, a journey of transformation that allows us to live an authentic life; one that we were created to live; one that is lived in faith, hope, and love; one that honors our spiritual and moral integrity; one that is expressed in intimacy, joy, peace, kindness, compassion, and generosity. By sharing and inviting you into my story, I pray that you will find elements in it that resonate for you and will, upon reflection, assist you in further developing and sustaining a more loving, enriching, meaningful, and hopeful spiritual life.

The Centrality of Hope

A life without hope is not, in the spiritual sense of the word, being completely alive. Instead, to live a life without hope is to live in the darkness of spiritual despair—where our perceptions of the world are filtered through the distorted lenses of resentment, pessimism, and cynicism. Existing without hope is having a life without a future. Erwin McManus writes, "Hope only exists in the future, and if the future does not exist there is no hope."[2] To exist in this dark place not only prevents us from enjoying life in the present but also prevents us from looking forward to everlasting union with God. A major aim of this book is to assist you in avoiding such an existence by helping you to understand how the voice of hope works in calling us to a spiritually enriching and fulfilling life.

With this purpose in mind, I wish to convey how hope plays an important role in our daily lives and how it can even empower and permit us to endure and accept indescribable pain and suffering. I wish to convey how hope is a blessing that invites us to cultivate a deeper and more enriching relationship with God.

Throughout the narrative of this book I will share with you how hope lives in many places, having many faces, expressions, and manifestations, both obvious and obscure. Expressions of hope are found in faith, love, prayer, celebrations, compassion, perseverance, courage, charity, and magnanimity. Less familiar to many of us is the idea that hope and hopefulness are also found in other places—diverse places such as pain and suffering, death and dying, truth, shame, guilt, regret, beauty, gratitude, forgiveness, service, and humility. By knowing where and how hope lives, we, like the good farmer who cultivates the soil to produce a rich harvest, can learn to cultivate a lifestyle that predisposes us to living in its fullness, wonder, and mystery.

> By knowing where and how hope lives, we, like the good farmer who cultivates the soil to produce a rich harvest, can learn to cultivate a lifestyle that predisposes us to living in its fullness, wonder, and mystery.

This book aspires to convey the reality that hope always exists, whether or not we recognize it, even in the midst of pessimism, apathy, fatalism, and our deepest despair, even in the midst of all the social, cultural, and moral unrest and ills of our time. I believe that hope, like love, rests in our souls. As Emily Dickinson puts it, hope is as "light as a feather." Hope can warm us in times of despair, transforming darkness into light, sadness into joy, fear into courage, and meaningless into purposefulness. Hope can also be experienced in the "chillest land"—throughout the world; in every nation, culture, and grouping; emanating from deep within our hearts, calling us to live in faith and love.

My Catholicism tells me that spiritual hope, along with faith and love, is a supernatural virtue and a gift from God that is infused in us as part of the fabric of our being, starting at the time of our conception. Josef Pieper teaches that the source of hope is in the "truly divine substance" in us, also known as grace. According to Piper, the "aim" of hope is directed at "supernatural happiness in God, who is known in a supernatural manner."[3] Furthermore, hope, like all virtues, calls us to live in spiritual purity, that is, in our interior goodness. In so doing, hope works silently, continuously, and diligently to keep us spiritually alive.

For me, to be spiritually alive is to live a meaningful life, one that is filled with love, joy, and purpose. To be spiritually alive also means not being self-centered but rather humble and centered on the concerns and well-being of others, our society, and the environment. When we are spiritually alive, we don't seek to possess but rather to be magnanimous; we don't live *for* the moment but rather live *in* the moment, enjoying life as we pass through the ordinary events of our daily existence.

I believe that the blessed triangle of faith, hope, and love work together by informing one another. Consequently, whether we recognize it or not, to live in faith is to live in love and hope, to live in hope is to live in faith and love, and to live in love–which St. Paul says is the greatest of the three—is to live in faith and hope. Also, whether we recognize it or not, these three supernatural virtues often live in mystery, working to influence and guide our lives beyond our conscience awareness or current understanding. For me, the guide through this landscape of mystery has been the Holy Spirit. I believe this Third Person of the Blessed Trinity has spoken to and been present in my life and will be part of the narrative of this book. The "inner voice" I will be referring to will be that of the Holy Spirit, a voice to which, through grace, I was listening and by which I was being guided.

Finally, although hope is future oriented, I've come to recognize that having hope is not asking us to live for the future. It is not asking us to put life on hold until things are better, completed, or fulfilled. To do so would prevent us from either finding meaning in our present circumstances or fully enjoying the richness the present holds. Instead, I have come to understand that hope allows us to rest patiently in the assurance that, no matter what circumstances we currently find ourselves in, the future will eventually be fine and will always offer us opportunities for peace, meaning and fulfillment. I have discovered that hope allows us to be *present to the present*—relaxing and taking pleasure in the richness that is continuously being offered to us while we wait for life to unfold.

Why This Book Now

This book is very timely, given the magnitude of negative forces and events that have impacted our world in these past several years. A combination of forces has put our entire planet in peril, fostering on a global scale feelings of fear, helplessness, misery, desolation, dejection, and hopelessness. Closer to home, the enormity of these prevailing feelings of disillusionment, disenchantment, and alienation are reflected in the latest statistics that indicate a steady rise of suicide in our youth and young adults, the time of life in which the next generation should be feeling hopeful and optimistic. However, we need only review the major natural disasters, acts of terrorism and genocide, wars, and financial scandals that dominate the headlines and network news to begin to understand why these prevailing negative feelings and attitudes exist.

Early in 2001, there was a scandal in which the Enron Corporation, the world's dominant energy trader, along with its accounting firm Arthur Anderson, deceived the investment world, causing millions of investors financial ruin. Also during that year, terrorism reached the shores of the United States on September 11 with the annihilation of the Twin Towers in Manhattan. This led to the "war on terrorism" and the invasion of Afghanistan and Iraq. These wars have resulted in the killing and maiming of hundreds of thousands, as well as in the incalculable devastation to population centers and landscapes in these countries. Over the past 15 years, we and other countries throughout the world have experienced flagrant pirating on the high seas, catastrophic wars, fires, earthquakes, tsunamis, hurricanes, cyclones, political assassinations, nuclear disasters, mass slaughtering, and persecutions and killing of innocent people. As if these calamities weren't sufficient, the ongoing weakness of the world economy has created an atmosphere of hate, mistrust, and pessimism regarding the ability of government to meet the financial, social, and environmental challenges with which we are faced.

Nevertheless, as I see it, in the midst of the devastating, catastrophic, and scandalous events—events that collectively have created unmitigated hardship, anguish, and despair to tens of millions here and around the world—the voice and face of hope was always there. Hope continues to provide light in the midst of all the darkness. Hope has been there to provide a life raft to those drowning in the sea of chaos, confusion, and uncertainty. Hope has been there to provide a blanket of comfort to those suffering from the loss of their loved ones, life savings, homes, and communities. Hope has been there to offer a badge of courage to those facing an uncertain and unpromising future. Through it all, hope has offered spiritual wisdom to those who have raised existential questions about the meaning behind their suffering, the meaning of their personal existence, the meaning of life itself.

> Through it all, hope has offered spiritual wisdom to those who have raised existential questions about the meaning behind their suffering, the meaning of their personal existence, the meaning of life itself.

For Whom This Book Was Written

This book reflects an integral part of my psychological well-being and spiritual journey. Indeed, the actual process of writing this work has been a major influence on my spiritual formation. However, my motivation for writing it has been my deep desire to serve and be of assistance to others. It was written for those seeking peace, solitude and a closer and more intimate relationship with God and their fellow human beings.

Also, although this book will reveal my life experiences, it is not my voice alone that will be heard. *Hope* is a collection of stories and an expression of the interior goodness of those who have had a major influence on my life. Accordingly, the book includes the voices and stories of those whom I love and serve, as well as the voices of many mentors, colleagues, and writers who have shared their wisdom with me.

In this introduction I am inviting you to journey with me through my story and the stories of those who have accompanied and influenced me. In accepting my invitation you will, as I have, discover the nature of hope, its various dimensions, and the multiple ways it manifests and expresses itself in our lives. You will discover and comprehend the various ways we can predispose ourselves to hope's fruits, as well as come to see how its presence can be recognized and celebrated. Armed with knowledge and awareness, you will make discoveries that will help you to embrace the loveliness of life, to live in love, joy, and gratitude, and to rest more deeply and peacefully in your true self and with the Divine Presence who dwells within, among, and around us.

Plan for This Book

As I have reflected on my life journey, I see that I have traveled through nine major periods to arrive where I am today. I have divided this book into those phases, but there really are no clear lines of demarcation separating them. Instead, like the seasons of the year, these periods transition from one into the other, with each phase shaping and influencing the next. Nevertheless, each phase represents a major turning point in my life and is marked by the particular themes that influenced my thoughts, feelings, behaviors, decisions, and choices at that stage of my journey. Each period portrays where I lived psychologically, emotionally, interpersonally, and spiritually at the time. Finally, for each phase, I describe how the Holy Spirit journeyed with me, offering me hope and a pathway to overcome the fears, struggles, and obstacles that life put in my path.

In Chapter 1, "Bathed in Warmth and Love," I describe how my being been raised as a young foster child by an African-American couple, Da and John, in the community of Watts in Los Angeles, influenced my long-term growth and development.

In Chapter 2, "Time of Loneliness and the Emergence of Shame," I tell of my return home to parents from whom I felt no love.

In Chapter 3, "Hope and Disillusionment," I share how I met and fell in love with Rosie, my wife of fifty years, and how she offered me a pathway out of the unhappiness and misery of my childhood.

Then, in Chapter 4, "Immersion in Guilt and Despair," I recount the abyss of desolation into which I was plunged when a priest told me in confession that, in order to receive absolution, I must leave my wife-to-be. In refusing his demand, I put myself into an emotional, psychological, and spiritual prison for the next twenty-four years, causing Rosie and me indescribable unhappiness for the first half of our marriage.

In Chapter 5, "My Vocation Finds Me," I explore how the Holy Spirit directed me into the social work profession and then used my career not only to serve the needs of others but also as an instrument for my own emotional and psychological transformation.

In Chapter 6, "Gift of Freedom," I explain how I eventually overcame my feelings of shame, ineptitude, and psychological insecurity.

Then, in Chapter 7, "Transformation from Religiosity to Spirituality," I describe how I traveled from despair and hopelessness to spiritual freedom, enlightenment, and an intimate relationship with Rosie and Our Lord.

In Chapter 8, "Evolution into a Spiritually Based Practitioner," I reflect on how my spiritual transformation guided me into becoming a spiritually based clinician.

In Chapter 9, "Caring for Souls," I show how the Holy Spirit called me into becoming a spiritual director.

In closing, I hope if you find this narrative interesting, enjoyable, and informative, you will stop and take the time to reflect upon anything—a word, phrase, or story—that draws your attention. I believe that if you are drawn to something, it is because your interior voice—the voice of your spirit—calls you to look deeper into its significance and meaning for your life. I also believe that what you discover will help increase your understanding of hope and enhance and enrich your relationship with God, your loved ones, and others you encounter throughout your life.

Chapter 1
Bathed in Warmth and Love

Emily

A child is born, her name is Emily
A gift to her parents, grandparents,
    and great-grandparents
A gift to all those who look upon her
A gift to the world

A child is born, her name is Emily
So gentle, peaceful, and beautiful
So filled with hopes and dreams
    yet to be fulfilled
So blessed by God with gifts, talents,
    and love

A child is born, her name is Emily
A manifestation of her parents' love
A manifestation goodness and joy
A manifestation of all that is wonderful
    and lovely in the universe

 I wrote the poem above as part of our family tradition of welcoming our grandchildren into the world. Emily is Eileen and David's second child, and in keeping with the birth of our grandchildren, we had a small family celebration and welcoming ceremony when she was a few days old. As my poem suggests, children are gifts not only to their parents but to all of us, and consequently we should all treasure them. They are blessings.

When I was born on October 25, 1943, I wasn't welcomed into such a warm and receptive atmosphere. As a child, I never felt loved by either of my parents. Because of the financial challenges they faced, I was placed as a two-year-old in a foster home. To shed light on how this came about, I must share with you a part of my parent's story.

My Parents Dream

In the early part of the 1900s, China was in the midst of a serious economic, political, and social crisis. My parents immigrated to the United States from China in the hope of finding a better life for themselves and the family they hoped to raise. Like most of their friends, they came to the United States as pioneers, and here they found themselves in an angry, hostile, and blatantly racist landscape. At that time, immigrants from China faced numerous discriminatory immigration policies. Among them were many obstacles that prevented them from becoming naturalized citizens. They also faced beatings, hangings, injustice in the courts, and laws that prevented them from entering most professions and businesses. In many states, like African Americans at the time, they weren't permitted to marry Caucasians.

As an adult, I have come to recognize, appreciate, and even admire the hardships my parents faced and overcame to provide me and my siblings the opportunities they themselves were denied. It wasn't until I wrote and delivered my father's eulogy that I recognized how I had helped to fulfill my parents' hopes and dreams, dreams they carried when they undertook their perilous journey across the Pacific.

Like many of those who made the same journey, my parents were poor, uneducated, and unskilled; they had to accept work wherever it was offered. For them it was in the grocery business. Just to make ends meet, they had to work long hours every day, leaving little time to adequately provide the care their children needed. They felt they had no alternative but to find foster homes for six of their children until they could bring us back home. I didn't know it at the time, but I was being blessed by the Holy Spirit when I was placed at age two in a loving home with Da and John, an African American couple living in the Watts area of Los Angeles.

The Blessings of Being Loved

I don't have any recollection of the house in Watts in which we lived or of the surrounding neighborhood. I do recall, however, that while living with Da and John I felt safe, warm, and loved. Although I only have a few memories of those early years, I carry them deep within the recesses of my heart and am always warmed by their recollection.

One special memory I have of that loving couple was the time when I was being bullied by one of the older children in the home. Da admonished the boy while holding, cuddling, and soothing me in her nurturing and embracing arms. Another precious memory is of the time I had a large blister on my leg that needed attending. I remember feeling scared and hurt, but John provided comfort while gently assuring me that I would be fine. I also have fond memories of their friends delighting in my presence. One gave me rides in his horse-drawn wagon while allowing me to hold the reins. I also recall the storekeeper of the local liquor store treating me with kindness and giving me candy when John lifted me onto his counter.

Later as a therapist, I learned the importance of these childhood events. When Da and John helped me to feel loved in the early formative years of my life, they and their friends significantly influenced my psychological, emotional, and spiritual formation. They planted within my interior landscape the seeds of hospitality, generosity, trust, and loving kindness—seeds that would eventually be given the opportunity to grow and blossom in me.

I was also to learn later that love and hope are inseparable, that where love exists, so does hope. Da and John's love implanted hope in my interior landscape. That hopefulness not only sustained me through the years of misery and despair that followed my time with them, but it also provided the courage to meet, challenge, and overcome the hardships in life I was called to face. Within this landscape of love and hope, I was later to recognize and claim the person God created me to be.

> What became the primary principle of my practice was to provide to those I serve a compassionate atmosphere, one in which they could feel safe, understood, respected, cherished, and hopeful.

Finally, I believe that my life with Da and John helped shape who I would become as a therapist. I know firsthand the importance of being nurtured as a child and the ways in which that nurturing is connected with long-term resilience and self-discovery. I am convinced that my ability to care for others was born in my experience with my foster parents. Furthermore, my life with them also taught me that a major contributing factor to many of my clients' psychological insecurities, poor self-esteem, and disrespect of themselves is the fact that as children they were treated with indifference, feeling invisible and unloved. What became the primary principle of my practice was to provide to those I serve a compassionate atmosphere, one in which they could feel safe, understood, respected, cherished, and hopeful. A second therapeutic principle of mine has been to convey that I see and recognize clients' talents, skills, strengths, and interior goodness. In providing such an environment and engaging in such a manner, I have seen them learn to acknowledge, claim, and embrace the lovely, caring, and beautiful person they were created to be.

Chapter 2
A Time of Loneliness
and the Emergence of Shame

> Love is patient; love is kind.
> Love is not jealous, it does not put on airs,
>   it is not snobbish.
> Love is never rude; it is not self-seeking,
> it is not prone to anger;
>   neither does it brood over injuries.
> Love does not rejoice in what is wrong
>   but rejoices with the truth.
> There is no limit to love's forbearance,
> To its trust, its hope, its power to endure.
>
>   1 Corinthians 13:4-7

 After returning home from Da and John's foster home, I never again saw my loving guardians. It took me a lot of effort as an adult to recover my memories of them. At the end of 1947, when I was four years old, my parents had the good fortune to borrow money from friends to build a grocery store and butcher shop in Lincoln Heights, a Mexican American community located in East Los Angeles. The design of the building provided sufficient living quarters on the second floor for all of us. It fulfilled my father's hopes and dreams, a place he could call home and raise his family.

I can only recall one time I visited my parents when I was living with Da and John. It was a horrible experience. I remember my mother had me sit by her at the dinner table and then scolded me for not liking and wanting to eat a particular dish. She forced it upon me anyway. When I left the dinner table, I couldn't keep it down. I threw up, soiling my clothes and making a mess on the floor. What I remember most is that I was punished for something over which I had no control.

A major turning point in my life was, of course, returning to my parents. My homecoming must have been an inauspicious occasion, because I have no memory of it. However, the first recollection I do have remains very vivid. My mother, with her pinched lips, angry eyes, and pointing finger, was scolding me for something that I cannot recall. I don't ever remember being treated by her with love, patience, or kindness. Instead, this form of engagement became the template and foundation for our relationship. This pattern of misbehaving, being scolded, and displeasing her continued throughout my childhood. This left me feeling inadequate, unwanted, and fearful. These feelings were so internalized that I used to believe that my parents found me in a trash bin and took me in. I guess at some level I thought I was a worthless piece of garbage. My deepest feelings about my home life for many years were those of loneliness, shame, and stupidity.

I vividly recall—and now fully understand—a later incident in which I was made to feel deeply ashamed of myself. The traumatizing occurrence took place in our playroom when I was about six. I was dancing and frolicking around to some music in my head when my mother caught me by surprise. Observing the way I was behaving, she scolded me while stating, *"Stop acting so stupid."* Later, as a therapist, I learned it was at that moment I was robbed of my childhood innocence. In other words, I was alienated from my interior beauty. My ability to spontaneously enjoy, participate in, and experience all the richness and goodness this world has to offer was lost. Feeling crushed and devastated by my mother's criticism, I immediately felt ashamed and wanted to hide. For the next thirty years I made every effort to do just that.

From that day forward, there were numerous times when I was made to feel the same way. Each incident deepened my negative perceptions of myself. There was, for example, the time when she was angry over the fact that I had to wear glasses, telling me it made me look stupid. From that time on, I was forbidden to put my glasses on in her presence. Or the times she scolded me because she frequently had to spend money to buy me new shoes. I was so afraid of her admonishments I would literally wear shoes until the soles fell off. Then I had to encounter the embarrassment of having to face the shoe salesperson in the awkward predicament of having obviously inadequate shoes and a mother complaining about having to buy me a new pair. These hurtful reoccurrences served to reinforce and deepen my traumatic wounds. This in turn led me to feel ashamed—not only of my behavior but also of myself. This evolved into my feeling fear of even being observed by others and contempt for my very existence.

At times, without me raising the issue, my mother would try to convey to me that she treated me the same as my siblings. In fact, that's what she said upon my graduation from high school when I told her and my dad that I had to leave them. I knew what she said wasn't true, and my siblings knew it as well. I can only assume that she believed what she was telling me. In any case, I left home right after high school with the feelings of being treated unfairly, unloved, and unwanted.

By and large, my relationship with my father was neutral. This is because I never spoke directly with him. My mother handled all matters regarding my behavior, particularly meting out the punishments for my supposedly all-too-frequent misconduct. For many years, I actually didn't know what my father thought or felt about me. There was, however, an incident that led me to believe that, like my mother, he didn't love me either. This happened when I accidently set our television on fire. After surveying the damage, he picked me up and, while giving me a spanking, angrily said, "Your mother is right. You're no good!" It wasn't the punishment that hurt, but his heart-piercing words. Not only were my feelings about how my mother felt towards me substantiated, but now I had "proof" that my dad felt the same way. I carried this misperception about my father's feelings for many years after leaving home.

The phrase "feeling lonely in a crowd" fit me perfectly at the time. Even though I was raised in a large family (I was the second youngest of eight children, with four brothers and three sisters), I have never developed a close relationship with any of my siblings. I'm not quite sure why, but it may, in part, be attributed to the fact that I was an introvert and shy and would rather listen to their conversations than join in on them.

Throughout my childhood I was so terrified of my parents that I only spoke with them in response to their questions or requests. I lived in such fear that I would do anything to hide and avoid being in their presence, even turning around and walking in another direction when I heard them speaking. Even today I harbor the insecurities I derived from our relationship, the fear of authority figures and of being judged, criticized, and admonished by others.

I spent hours as a child dwelling on why my parents didn't love me. I could only conclude that I was either defective or must have done something terribly wrong, but I didn't know what it was. I also spent hours sitting mute and feeling lonely in the corner of our large living room, observing and listening to my siblings interacting without joining in. At dinner, which always began promptly at 7:00 p.m., I sat frightened and mute next to my mother, never entering any of the family conversations. Making matters worse, she often required that I eat foods that I detested. To find some measure of safety and comfort, I would lie in bed snuggling up against the wall, tightly wrapped in my warm blanket. Maybe this is why today—at the age of seventy—I still enjoy and take consolation in lingering in bed when I wake up in the morning.

Two Friends

I was not allowed to socialize outside of school, so my closest "friend" in those years was the television set. Nonetheless, I was fortunate to establish one long-lasting friendship at that time. I met Art in the second grade. We played together at school and whenever I was able to sneak out of the house on Sunday afternoons when my parents left to socialize with their friends. This deception was supported by my sister Liz, who was responsible for overseeing me and my siblings Chester, Douglas, and Elaine. In many respects Art became more like a brother than my actual family members. In addition to sharing countless adventures, he taught me various sports, how to ride a bike, and eventually how to drive a car. The impact of my close human connection with Art has had a profound effect on my life.

At the deepest level, Art offered me a ray of hope that life could be enriching. I always anticipated and look forward to our meetings. As adolescents we solidified our friendship through the ritual of becoming blood brothers. Not only were we best men at each other's weddings, I later became godfather to his eldest son Mitchell. For the past sixty years, the rhythms of our lives have been so spiritually intertwined that, even though we seldom see each other anymore, when we do it is as though not a day has passed since our last conversation.

My other friend as a child, the television set, provided me companionship and entertainment. My parents were uneducated working class people who wanted us to be successful, but they had no awareness of how to point us in that direction. Through no fault of their own, they didn't encourage their children to read or participate in any of the fine arts. I spent countless hours watching mindless TV programs and didn't develop an interest in literature, music, or art until much later in my life.

Daydreams: A Sign of Hope

During this unhappy period of my life, I unknowingly encountered another experience of hopefulness. This took the form of daydreaming. To mitigate my misery, I immersed myself in various daydreams, two of which stand out. The first was the hope of buying a blue Triumph sports car and driving it with the top down through a beautiful forest (I later fulfilled this dream). This image was a replica of an advertisement I had seen on television. The second daydream involved visiting America's national parks. I had fallen in love with nature films somehow, and as a consequence I wanted to immerse myself in the beauty and grandeur of the outdoors. My thoughts included images of outdoor camping, backpacking in Yosemite National Park, and rafting down the Colorado River in the middle of the Grand Canyon (all of which I eventually did).

It wasn't until years later, in my work as a therapist, that I discovered the reason for this curious avocation and its influence on my spiritual formation. I came to understand that unlike fantasies, which are attempts to escape from the world, daydreams are manifestations of hopefulness. They are symbols and products of our inner essence looking to the future to express itself and be fulfilled. To illustrate, my daydream of driving through the forest in a Triumph with the top down represented the joyful, playful, and free-spirited side of myself that was not allowed to find expression under my parents' care. Likewise, my dream of visiting and camping in national parks represented my sense of adventure, intellectual curiosity, appreciation of natural beauty, and connection with the Divine Presence. To daydream is to live in the present and in the "not-yet" dimensions of life at the same time, to live in the hope of realizing in the future those things that we sense would enrich our lives, affirm our interior goodness, and give true meaning to our existence. As Erwin McManus writes in *Soul Cravings*, "Our dreams are where God paints a picture of a life waiting to be created."[1]

The Call to Faith

The Columban's, an Irish missionary order of the Catholic Church, were expelled from China when the communists began governing the country. In order to continue serving the Chinese, they established missions in large Chinese communities in the United States, one being in the Chinatown area of Los Angeles. My two oldest siblings, Evelyn and Martin, became involved in St. Bridget's, the name the Columbans gave to their place of worship. Evelyn and Martin converted to Catholicism a short time later. In 1955, when I was twelve, they asked and received permission from my parents to have me formally convert as well. I'm sad to say that my conversion wasn't because of any real interest in God but rather because it provided me with a respite from my parents. This isn't to say that I didn't believe in God at the time of my baptism, but I wasn't really aware of the true meaning and significance of the path upon which I was embarking.

Years later, I learned that my conversion was the Holy Spirit at work, inviting me into the Church. And by accepting the Spirit's invitation, even for the wrong reasons, I had unknowingly become a pilgrim on a mysterious journey into faith, love, and hope—a personal and mystical journey that many spiritual writers say we were created to travel. The Holy Spirit would reveal to me over the passage of time my destiny and the many secrets my life journey has revealed.

Nevertheless, at the time converting to Catholicism was actually a double-edged sword for me. On one side, I could take some comfort in the belief that I was on a path that could lead me to heaven, but on the other it amplified and reinforced my psychological insecurities and deepened my feelings of guilt and shame.

Thomas Keating writes that the Catholic Church at that time (the 1950s) espoused a Western model of spirituality. This model emphasized external acts as being more important than internal ones and urged that we initiate good works only because of God's immediate rewards for doing so. It emphasized an overarching concern about getting to heaven rather than exercising the love of God and neighbor in the here and now. Furthermore, the emphasis was on God being somewhere outside of ourselves, dictating laws and passing judgments. In short, it underscored a theology of fear, Hell, and damnation, a theology of absolute obedience to the magisterium, the Church's teaching authority, and a theology of a God that was somewhere in the heavens looking down and ready to banish us to the burning fires of Hell for all eternity if we committed just one unforgiven *mortal* or serious sin.

My knowledge of the Church and of God was acquired through indoctrination rather than through the process of questioning, exploration, and discovery. I was required to memorize the *Baltimore Catechism*, which gave simple answers to all the significant questions regarding the faith I was proposing to join. For example, the question: Who is God? The answer: God is the Supreme Being who made things. Or, the question: Why did God make us? The answer: God made us to know, love, and serve him in this world and to be happy with him in the next. We were taught that Catholicism was the one and only true faith and, under the risk of committing a serious sin, we were forbidden to attend other churches, read anything that challenged the Church's authority or teachings, or see films that might corrupt our thoughts and feelings. To insure our innocence, the Church maintained and distributed a list of its banned readings and movies. These restrictions even applied to Church theologians and scriptural scholars. This Church environment in which I was raised didn't encourage curiosity, self-reflection, and spiritual growth. Instead, the theology in which I was raised could be summarized in three words, "pray, pay, and obey," with the inherent message being that you would be punished if you didn't do what you were told.

In such a castigatory climate, I learned to love God with my head, not my heart, a love predicated on a definition given to me without the accompanying feelings of comfort and intimacy. My love for God was servile, founded on fear of Hell and damnation if I didn't follow the Church's teachings, rather than filial, founded on gratitude and fidelity and based on the recognition of how much God cares for us with his infinite love. Instead of living in spiritual warmth and freedom, I lived in the constant fear that any serious violation of the Ten Commandments might put my eternal existence in jeopardy. God forbid if I masturbated, had a lewd thought, or stole a candy bar from my parents' store! I actually believed that I might be condemned to Hell for all time for any of these transgressions.

As a consequence of my early Catholic upbringing, I became very scrupulous, always second-guessing my honesty and motives when asking for forgiveness in the confession box. Was I truly being sincere, truly feeling contrite for my transgressions? Were my sins venial and minor or mortal and deadly? Was I being honest when I was asked to say my act of contrition or do the penance that the priest gave me? These questions plagued and disturbed me for the next twenty-five years. Often, like an addict after taking a fix, I would, upon leaving the confessional, have a sense of emotional relief. I believed that I was *pure* and going to heaven. But shortly afterwards I would violate another commandment (always in a very minor way) and begin obsessing and living in fear over having again put my soul in peril.

My understanding of hope in these early years was only associated with redemption and salvation after death. I was taught to believe that the sacrifice of Jesus Christ on the cross redeemed me from original sin and that Baptism and following God's teachings would liberate me from my sinful nature, save my soul, and earn me a place in heaven. As I understood it, the theology behind such hope was primarily concerned with life after death rather than living in the richness, warmth, and contentment of the present. Because of my scrupulosity, such hope afforded me little comfort. Instead this pre-Vatican Council II theology perpetuated in me feelings of fear and living in a psychological, emotional, and spiritual penitentiary.

Even though I was terribly unhappy as a teenager, it was during this period that I was graced by my first mystical experience. This beautiful and loving encounter caught me completely by surprise. It happened while I was attending Mass and listening to the gospel on the Sermon on the Mount near my home at The Church of the Sacred Heart in LA. During the Scripture readings, I suddenly felt I was being transported before Christ and that he was speaking directly to me. I also felt I was being bathed in the Divine Presence. Feeling overwhelmed with comfort and joy, I began crying hysterically. For the moment, I felt God's celestial love enveloping my entire being. My feelings, however, were short-lived, dissipating shortly after leaving the church. Nevertheless, unbeknown to me at the time, the seeds of hope and contemplation had been planted deep within the recesses of my heart.

Although the prevailing spiritual mood during this period of my life was fear and anxiety, my faith did have its fruits. I enjoyed and was enriched by the rituals of the Catholic Church, especially attendance at Mass and receiving Holy Eucharist. The Church's celebration of the Christmas season was also significant for me. I took seriously this festive occasion and embraced with my heart the birth of Christ. In so doing, I was immersed in the feelings of love, joy, warmth, and hopefulness that permeate the air during this beautiful season.

The Deepening of Shame

In addition to my conversion to Catholicism and the unfortunate consequence of being burdened with guilt and the fear of being condemned to burning in Hell, there were two other major experiences during my early years that cultivated, extended, and intensified my sense of shame. These experiences also shaped the way

I thought, felt, and behaved through much of my young adult life. The first incident, and another turning point, came about while in the eighth grade in Ms. Jean Beauvoir's social studies class. To compensate for my feelings of not feeling wanted or even noticed at home, I drew attention to myself in school by hiding behind the role of the class clown. During one of my obnoxious and disruptive moments, Ms. Beauvoir admonished me before the entire class, reinforcing my already deep feelings of stupidity and shame. I felt so shocked and traumatized by the experience that I retreated deeper into my self-imposed internal hiding place by literally losing my voice in class. From that moment forward, I refused to speak in a classroom setting. The fear of exposing myself and being ridiculed before an audience plagued me well into my thirties. I had not only been robbed of my innocence but also robbed of my ability to speak out. Furthermore, I was now caught in a double bind, on the one hand wanting to be recognized and appreciated but on the other afraid to draw any attention to myself for fear of being ridiculed.

The second significant experience during this period was having to attend four years of Chinese school. The goal of the school wasn't to teach English as a second language but to enhance the students' reading and writing skills in Chinese. None of the instructors spoke English, and unlike me, the other students already knew the Chinese language. I was constantly admonished and punished for speaking with the students next to me in order to try to understand what was being said by the instructors. I was, once again, made to feel stupid and ashamed for circumstances over which I had no control. These feelings were reinforced every time I couldn't respond to my parents' friends when they spoke to me in Chinese.

The Planting of Seeds

Attending Abraham Lincoln Junior and Senior High School, where 90 percent of the student population was Mexican-American, offered another formative experience in my life during this time. It was here that I met Mr. Raymond Lopez, a warm, kind, and caring man who took me under his wing, providing me with the care, support, and understanding for which I longed. He became my first mentor, and for six years he planted in me the seeds of leadership. Throughout my tenure at school, Mr. Lopez helped me acquire the knowledge and skills to become a student leader, which culminated in my being elected student body president.

The time spent at Lincoln was rich and satisfying. I was involved in a variety of extracurricular activities and participated actively in sports. In addition, I enjoyed the friendship of a small circle of intimate friends I remain connected with today. However, I struggled in the classroom, earning only passing grades that served to reinforce my feelings of shame and stupidity. Beneath the façade of being popular, I continued to feel inferior, inadequate, and ashamed of myself, believing in my heart that if my friends *really* knew me I would be ridiculed and rejected by them.

Thus my six-year experience at Lincoln established a paradoxical pattern that would follow me well into my adulthood. On one hand was a caring voice like that of Mr. Lopez, who provided me with kindness, support, validation, and a hope that I was worthwhile and could be successful in life. But on the other hand were the overriding voices of my mother and my grade-school teacher, Ms. Jean Beauvoir, who kept me smothered, even in the face of my accomplishments, in feelings of doubt, confusion, stupidity, and worthlessness.

Crisis and Opportunity

Experiencing the unhappiness in my childhood, and observing as a therapist the devastating impact major disasters, personal tragedies, and abusive or neglectful relationships can have on us, has led me to believe that there is nothing inherently good in such events, circumstances, or relationships. Through my own experiences and listening to the stories of those I serve, however, I have also come to believe in the miracle that good can be derived from mishaps, catastrophes, and misfortunes—if we are willing to do the work necessary to understand and digest them.

In the Chinese language, the character for crisis is the same character as opportunity. I now believe that, like the mythical phoenix—who is miraculously reborn after dying and bursting into ashes, stronger, lovelier, and more beautiful than ever before—that we all have the ability to transform the burnt ashes of our lives into elements of goodness. This transformation can comfort our bodies, heal our emotional wounds, nurture our souls, prepare us for whatever the future holds, and restore our peace and tranquility. The Sufi story of "Fatima the Spinner and the Tent," found in Shah's *Tales of the Dervishes*, gives credence to this belief.

The young woman in the story, Fatima, had to face three catastrophic, devastating, and life-altering events in her life before finding the security, peace, and love for which she so dearly longed. She lived comfortably before leaving with her father on a business trip to the islands of the Middle Sea to sell their merchandise. They happened to be prosperous spinners. While sailing to Crete, a storm blew up and the ship was wrecked. Her father was killed. Fatima found herself alone, destitute, and utterly exhausted on the shore near Alexandria. She was found wandering the sands by a family of cloth makers who took her in and taught her their craft. Within a few years, she found herself temporarily happy and content with her new life. But one day while Fatima was walking on the seashore, a band of slave-traders landed and carried her away with their other captives. Feeling miserable and dejected, she was taken to Istanbul and sold as a slave.

Fatima was bought by a kindly man, a maker of masts for ships, to work as a serving-maid for his wife. A few years later, however, the couple lost an investment of all their wealth in a cargo captured by pirates. Since her master could no longer afford workers, he and his wife and Fatima were left alone to work at the heavy labor of making masts. As they worked together, Fatima was befriended by the couple, given her freedom, and became relatively happy in her third career.

During a trip to Java to sell the masts they had made, the ship upon which Fatima was sailing was wrecked off the coast of

China. Once again, Fatima found herself alone, destitute, and in despair in a strange land. It so happened that there was a search under way to find a foreign woman who would fulfill the prophecy of making a tent for the emperor. Found by local villagers, Fatima was taken before him to discover whether she was the one. Using the knowledge and skills she had acquired being a spinner, weaver, and wood-fashioner, Fatima was able to make the necessary ropes, stout cloth, and tent poles to construct the tent the emperor desired. As a consequence of pleasing him, she was granted her wish of marrying a prince and remaining in China, where she lived happily with her family for the rest of her life.

The moral of this story is evident, as is my visceral reaction to it. Our journey in life is a journey into uncertainty and mystery, and even if we are destined to pass through negative, depressing, despairing, and even catastrophic occurrences, there is always the hope that the lessons learned from these experiences can somehow instill wisdom, strengthen our character, prepare us for whatever the future holds, and lead us into discovering enriching and fulfilling lives.

I now recognize that many of the fears, insecurities, and adaptive behaviors that I internalized in childhood have been transformed or evolved into strengths that now contribute to my understanding of interpersonal relationships. I now recognize, as I will share in a later chapter, how my painful experiences in life have had a major influence on my psychological, professional, and spiritual transformation.

I am not suggesting that God put in my path the adversities and challenges I faced in order to shape and transform me into who and what I am today. I don't believe God intervenes in our lives in such a manipulative manner. Instead, I believe God has given us the gift of free will—a gift that allows us to live in freedom, a gift that allows us to make judgments and decisions regarding the direction of our lives.

The circumstances in which I was raised and the challenges I had to face were not created or caused by God. Instead, the liability and responsibility lies with the judgments and decisions of those who injured me, as well as with my own judgments and decisions. However, I do believe that the Holy Spirit has always been my companion, mysteriously guiding me through the trials I have had to face. I believe the Spirit has been assisting me in challenging and overcoming the fears and insecurities in which I was immersed. I believe the Spirit has been working within the recesses of my soul in helping me to recognize that my insecurities could be transformed into insights, my weaknesses into strengths, my stupidity into wisdom, my shame into sensitivity, and my fears into courage. In short, I don't believe God causes our problems but instead, through the intercessions of the Holy Spirit working mysteriously within the recesses of our souls, is there to help us find a path to face and overcome them.

Chapter 3
Hope and Disillusionment

The Third Body

A man and a woman sit near each other;
As they breathe they feed someone
 we do not know,
Someone we know of, whom we have
 never seen....
They obey a third body that they share
 in common.
They have promised to love that body.

ROBERT BLY

 I cannot separate the story of my spiritual journey from my relationship with Rosie, my loving companion of fifty years. I have shared with her on many occasions that she has been one of God's most precious gifts to me. We now rest in the beauty, intimacy, and spirituality expressed in Robert Bly's poem above, found in Roger Housden's book *Ten Poems to Open Your Heart*. Like the characters in Bly's beautiful poem, Rosie and I now share a "third body" in the peace and comfort of just being ourselves, in being enriched by the activities we enjoy, and in being fulfilled by the presence of each other in the ordinary course of our lives. This includes, among other things, in spending time on walks, in visiting our children and their families, and in celebrating festive occasions. We know we are accepted by others for being ourselves, and we accept ourselves as such. We know that our love transcends time and space and that the rhythms of our lives are intricately and mysteriously interwoven, connected, and experienced–even when we are physically apart. We know we rest in the trust and shelter of each other's spirit. We know we are soul mates.

As my story unfolds, however, you will learn that our marriage hasn't been easy. It seems to me illuminating that our relationship followed the same path that my personal and spiritual travels took: in the beginning being bathed in love; followed by a long period in which Rosie and I lived in the abyss of alienation, frustration, and despair; but in the end rediscovering the love, intimacy, and goodness that we initially enjoyed and do so to this day. Thanks be to God we were able to find solutions to the many impediments and obstacles that were placed in our path, including painful separations.

In my struggle to overcome the emotional scars of my early childhood and problems with my faith, I for years projected, displaced, blamed, in short, dumped my anger, resentments, and insecurities onto her. Rosie, in turn, never wavered from her love and devotion towards me. She was always working actively to support my education, career, ambitions, and spiritual needs and was always there for me, especially when I was in a midst of a crisis and needed her most.

A Time of Enchantment

Even though I know we were destined to be together, I admit the beginning of my life with Rosie was inauspicious and disappointing. My older brother Pete, who knew her brother Jack, introduced us in her parent's apartment when we were just sixteen. I recall her sitting in her parent's rocking chair with her hair pinned in large rollers and her face covered with white cleansing cream. She was dressed in a white blouse and tight fitting black and white checkered pants. I don't know what she thought of me, but I immediately found her unattractive and after the exchange of a few pleasantries made up some excuse to leave. Before returning to our car I told my brother, "Please don't do me any more favors."

I hadn't planned to see Rosie again, but two months later at one of her school dances at Belmont High she came up to me and reintroduced herself. I found myself unexpectedly anxious, out of breath, and—to my surprise—moonstruck. I had fallen in love at second sight. We spent the remainder of our time together constantly being reminded by the teachers that we were dancing too closely. Shortly thereafter we agreed to go steady, which led to spending endless hours talking on the telephone, sending dedications and messages to local disc jockeys to broadcast professions of our love, and meeting whenever I could sneak out. I eventually enrolled in summer school at Belmont so we could be together. I recall being so enamored that I didn't even bother eating at the school's family association's annual Kow Kong picnic.

Being lost in love overshadowed my feelings of misery at home. Until I met Rosie, I had been held and comforted only once since leaving Da and John, and that was by my sister Liz. Now I had found the girl who would love, nurture, comfort, and rescue me from my loneliness and feelings of being unwanted. I had found the girl who would offer me hope for a loving and enriching future. I had found the girl who could make me feel special and happy. Although my love for Rosie was real, I learned later that I was also living in a fantasy, that making her responsible for my happiness was an unrealistic expectation. I learned through therapy that happiness must come from within and cannot be made the responsibility of another. I unknowingly used Rosie to meet my selfish and insecure needs. Nevertheless, over the next two years I lived in a world full of dreams, a world filled with inspiring, fulfilling, and hopeful moments.

Leaving the Nest

I was feeling happy throughout my later high school years, especially enriched by my relationship with Rosie. However, another major disheartening incident with my mother instigated another turning point in my life. It happened when my sister Liz told her that I had been elected student body president, to which my mother responded, "All he is trying to do is show off." I was devastated when I heard of her response. Angrily I told Mr. Lopez that I wanted to decline the presidency, that it was meaningless. I changed my mind reluctantly only after my mentor convinced me that I had an obligation to the school and those who had elected me.

I now recognize that I was hoping my high school accomplishments would make my parents feel proud of me and show some appreciation of me. My mother's heart-piercing comment made it completely evident that there was nothing I could do to receive any positive recognition from them. I decided that leaving home was the only solution to alleviating my misery. What I didn't know at the time was that implicit in my decision to leave home was the hope I could somehow find recognition and acceptance somewhere else.

I was able to follow through with my escape plan thanks to my brother Pete and his wife, Hazel, who agreed to provide a place for me to stay until I became self-sufficient, and my brother Chester, who found employment for me as a stock boy where he worked. When I met with my parents to inform them that I felt unwanted and therefore had to leave, my mother reiterated what she had always said to me throughout the years: "You think I don't like you, but I treat all my children the same." As usual, her words felt empty and only reinforced my feelings of being unloved. My father on the other hand, surprised me by crying and saying,

"Why do you think I've been working so hard? I want you to have a better life than me." His words also brought tears to my eyes, and in that wonderful moment I felt loved by him. It was such an indescribably beautiful experience, something that I would never have imagined happening. I didn't respond to either of them. Even though I discovered by father's true feelings towards me, I couldn't continue to live in fear and misery and left home immediately after graduating from high school.

Upon leaving home, I found a new sense of freedom that I had never experienced. Within the reasonable rules set by Pete and Hazel, I could come and go as I pleased. I enjoyed my work and spent a great amount of time visiting with Rosie, reveling in all the richness that a loving relationship has to offer. In addition, I began attending Los Angeles Junior College in the evening, working toward a degree that would allow me to teach history in high school. My prevalent feelings during this period were those of freedom, happiness, satisfaction, and hopefulness. I felt safe and supported living with my brother and sister-in-law, was in a loving relationship, enjoyed my work, and was planning and working towards a future to which I looked forward.

Separation and Renewal

Approximately seven months after I left home, however, Rosie and I decided to separate, believing that we were too young to make a long term commitment and that we needed more experience at dating. Although difficult, we knew it was the reasonable and mature thing to do. But we were destined to be together, and a few months later fate entered our lives, creating the opportunity for our hearts to be reunited. This happened when a planned double date with my closest friends Art and Maria fell through. When we arrived to the home of Naomi, the girl who was supposed to be my date, I was informed by her mother that Naomi had been trying to reach me because something had unexpectedly interfered with her plans. Instead of taking me home, Art and Maria insisted I give Rosie a call. Besides being in the neighborhood, they had fond feelings for her. Reluctantly, I acquiesced. Rosie was pleasantly surprised to receive my call and, because her feelings towards me hadn't changed, readily said yes to my invitation. We all drove to Pacific Ocean Park.

It was an enchanting day. It felt as though a second hadn't passed since our last meeting. We laughed with joy while high in the sky on the Ferris wheel, held hands on the merry-go-round, and lovingly shared a hamburger and coke from one of the concession stands. Imbedded in my heart is the moment when we embraced and kissed at the end of the park's pier. It was a *mystical* experience: We were totally absorbed in the beauty of our love. In that moment, I knew without a doubt that I wanted to be with her for the rest of my life. Eventually, she and I made plans to marry after we graduated from college and, as our love continued to grow, we became lovers.

I couldn't have felt more happy and hopeful with the direction that my life had taken. I had everything I ever wanted—independence; enriching friendships, a loving, intimate, and joyful relationship, and a hope-filled future. It was a magical period. I discovered the meaning of love, felt its endearing and enriching influence, and developed an awareness of how it transforms the way we perceive and engage in our world. I was transported out of myself and immersed into all the wonder, loveliness, and mystery that life has to offer. Absorbed in this cosmology of love, I developed an awareness of beauty that both surrounded and was within me. Everything appeared enhanced. Foods seemed more tasteful, the colors of flowers looked more vibrant, and my friendships felt more intimate.

> I discovered the meaning of love, felt its endearing and enriching influence, and developed an awareness of how it transforms the way we perceive and engage in our world.

All seemed to be well in the world, until like in the story of Fatima the spinner, a major catastrophe stripped me of my new life and, with it, all my hopes and dreams. Tossed once again into the hopelessness of disillusionment, I would come to understand the negative side of love, not negative in the sense of "bad," but rather what complements love's positive dimensions. My feelings of intimacy would turn into grief and my feelings of joy into sadness. Only later would I come to understand the complementary relationship between these experiences. I would also learn that because they are dimensions of love they are also manifestations of hope.

Chapter 4
Immersion into Guilt and Despair

How lovely is your dwelling place, O Lord of hosts!
My soul longs, indeed it faints
   for the courts of the Lord;
my heart and my flesh sing out for joy
   to the living God.

Even the sparrow finds a home,
    and the swallow a nest for herself,
    where she may lay her young
at Your altars, O Lord of hosts,
my King and my God.
Happy are those who live in your house;
    ever singing your praise.

Happy are those whose strength is in you,
    in whose heart are the highways to Zion.
As they go through the valley of Baca
    they make it a place of springs;
    the early rain also covers it with pools.
They go from strength to strength;
    the God of Gods will be seen in Zion.

O LORD of God of hosts, hear my prayer;
> give ear, O God of Jacob!
Behold our shield, O God;
> look upon the face of your anointed.
For a day in Your courts is better
> than a thousand elsewhere.
I would rather be a doorkeeper
> in the house of my God
> than live in the tents of wickedness.
For the LORD God is a sun and shield;
> he bestows favor and honor.
No good thing does the LORD withhold
> from those who walk uprightly.
O LORD of hosts,
> happy is everyone who trusts in you.

PSALM 84

I love the imagery this prayerful psalm elicits and the invitation it offers. To be welcomed and invited in the sanctuary of God's home to nest and be comforted by his infinite love is such a precious gift. But the guardians and doorkeepers of his house at this time in my spiritual formation weren't presenting such a message. Instead of teaching me that I was unconditionally welcome in God's kingdom, I was taught I had to deserve an invitation. God's love was presented to me as conditional, that I had to earn it by avoiding sins, and only then would I be invited to rest in the warmth and safety of his tabernacle. Besides, God's home was not here on earth but somewhere in a mysterious place called "heaven." What might be considered his earthly home and sanctuary, his Church, was not for me a place of kindness and hospitality but rather a place of unfriendliness and aloofness; not a place for heartfelt worship but a place where I went each Sunday to meet a religious obligation; a place in which I was not presented with homilies on spiritual growth but lectures on sin and obedience; not a place where I could be reconciled and reunited with our compassionate Lord but a place I went to confession to prevent being damned to the fires of Hell.

Instead of fostering trust in God's infinite compassion in me, the Church fostered fear. Instead of guiding me on a path laden with what it calls the fruits of the spirit (those being love, joy, peace, patience, kindness, gentleness, faithfulness, discipline, and generosity), the Church enslaved me in rigid rules and regulations. Instead of providing me with comfort and understanding, the church commanded me to listen and obey. Before I could discern the meaning of Psalm 84, that God's home is here on earth, that his love is unconditional, that he invites everyone, not just Catholics, to rest in his Garden of Eden, I had to discover a way out of the hurricane and swirling chaos of spiritual despair, confusion, and bleakness in which I was swept up. I had to find a path out of the darkness of ignorance, blindness of naïveté, and prison of insecurity.

My Journey into Despair

In the previous chapter I shared how Rosie and I met, fell in love, and were looking forward to being happily married. My dream turned into a nightmare. We were married, but the day of our wedding was the most miserable day of my life. This unfortunate turn of events began when, feeling guilty for our having become lovers before the wedding, I went to confession. The priest to whom I was confessing denounced our relationship vehemently, even though I informed him that we were in love and planning to marry. He went on to say that I was living an immoral and sinful life and that my connection with Rosie was based solely on lust. He instructed me to end it under the penalty of not being given absolution. I pleaded with him without success to change his perception of our relationship. Knowing what I felt towards Rosie to be true, I couldn't deny our love and walked out of the confessional. But not receiving absolution had a devastating, disillusioning, and traumatic effect on me. The happy future I was looking forward to and planning was ripped out of my heart. My feelings of hopefulness were transformed into feelings of chaos, despair, and guilt.

In retrospect I recognized that I had violated a morale code I said I believed in: to not engage in premarital sex. The priest would have been correct in requiring me to stop. But he was exceeding his prerogative in unequivocally stating that my connection with Rosie was based solely on lust. He was in a position to judge the sinful acts (sex outside of marriage) but in no position to judge what was in our hearts. His misjudgment led to a failed confession and the lack of reconciliation to grace. It also led to my guilt feelings associated with my perceived misbehavior. Most devastatingly, it took the beauty of our love and turned it into something that was presented to me as immoral and despicable. My hope of having an enriching marriage was suddenly transformed into despair, confusion, and misery.

> My hope of having an enriching marriage was suddenly transformed into despair, confusion, and misery.

At the time I believed at face value and without question what I was told by leaders of the Church. I believed by not following the priest's instruction I was condemned to the fires of Hell. After all, it said in John's Gospel that the Lord said to his disciples, "Receive the Holy Spirit. If you forgive the sins of any, they are forgiven them; if you retain the sins of any, they are retained" (John 20:22-23). I was caught in a spiritual koan, the answer to which wasn't revealed to me until it nearly destroyed me and my marriage. On one hand I loved and had promised to marry Rosie, and on the other I had promised to love and obey God. It appeared impossible to honor one promise without breaking the other. Caught in this paradox, I was emotionally paralyzed and didn't know where to turn.

Eventually I turned to Rosie to rescue me from my dilemma. I told her about what had happened and explained that the only way I could receive absolution and not go to Hell was to end our relationship. Rather than taking the responsibility upon myself, I asked her to make the decision for me. I believed that if she truly loved me she would let me go. Instead of sending me away, however, Rosie bravely told me that the priest was wrong and that if the relationship was to end, I would have to make the decision. I just couldn't find it in my heart to hurt and abandon her. And so we were married.

I didn't know it at the time, but the despair, confusion, and sadness I was experiencing were not from feeling damned but were associated with having been emotionally torn away from the person I loved. Rosie wasn't dead, but might as well have been. The Church had placed her beyond my emotional and spiritual reach. This crazy situation lasted for the first couple of decades of our marriage. Finally, through the grace and mysterious workings of the Holy Spirit, our hearts were reunited twenty-three years later, transforming the underlying sadness that had permeated our marriage until then into the endless joy we hoped for and experienced in our youth.

Before the wedding, Rosie became pregnant. I believe now that her pregnancy wasn't accidental, that I unconsciously wanted to this to happen. It would be the solution to my moral dilemma because the Church would want me to do the right thing and marry her. At the time, I couldn't see the hypocrisy of this logic. It may have resolved my immediate moral problem, but Rosie's pregnancy led me further into feelings of guilt, created major conflicts in our relationship, eroded my love, and cast serious doubts regarding my wish to be married. It also led me to put up an invisible barrier between us, one that wasn't completely removed for two decades. On May 8, 1964, I betrayed her by marrying her out of guilt and a sense that I was doing the right thing rather than out of love, freedom, and joy. I took no responsibility for my betrayal and for years blamed her for my misery. In fact it was me who created our miserable state of marital affairs.

Rosie has always loved me unconditionally and was happy on the day of our wedding. But I knew in my heart of hearts that I lied when we exchanged our vows. Instead of my wedding being the happiest occasion in my life, as I had envisioned in my youth, it was the worst. Throughout the day, I was moody, upset, and miserable, and in the evening I managed to pick an argument with my bride. I had locked us into a prison of mistrust, chaos, and misery. In subsequent months, I continued to question whether I loved her and if I had only married her out of guilt or obligation. In the midst of my confusion, our son Richard was born six months after the wedding.

Shame and Guilt

For the longest time I was caught in a double whammy. My mother had imprisoned me in the feelings of shame and guilt. I learned later that there is healthy shame which is caused by violating a family, community, or cultural code of conduct and that such shame guards against narcissism and arrogance. But the shame I experienced here was not based on my misbehavior. Rather I was made to feel ashamed of my very being and existence. I also learned later that there is healthy guilt, which is feeling bad for violating our moral code and that such guilt guards against immorality; but that priest made me feel guilty for things I shouldn't have felt guilty about. As a result, I thought—because these feelings made me feel so bad—that I was bad in my essence.

Later, as a therapist, I learned the difference between healthy and unhealthy shame and guilt and that the former are gifts of the Holy Spirit and play an important role in influencing and shaping our moral character. Although they elicit the painful feelings of remorse, regret, and contrition, these feelings remind us that we are violating our spiritual integrity and provide a path towards renewal, restoration, and interior transformation, a path that may require making restitution for the hurt and damage that we may have inflicted. They also cultivate humility, reminding us we are no different from our fellow human beings in our ability to exercise poor judgment, be controlled by our fears, and injure others. They challenge us to honor our interior goodness by taking responsibility for our inappropriate thoughts, feelings, and actions. They alert us to the fact that we may be heading in a direction that alienates us from ourselves and God. Of utmost importance, these feelings are gifts that continue to offer us the hope that we can always redirect our lives in a manner that allows us to live in, peace, integrity and authenticity.

I felt extremely guilty after realizing that I betrayed Rosie on the day of our wedding and was the cause of so much of her pain, suffering, and misery through the early years of our marriage. As it turned out, my guilt was the blessing that not only led me to recapture my authenticity but also led me to finally apologize and ask for her forgiveness. My guilt was transformed into the substance that moved and continues to move me to provide her with a safe home in which she can rest in warmth, comfort, and love. We are now able to fulfill the hopes and dreams of our youth. Finally, I was to learn later that my guilt was also transformed into humility, becoming part of the foundation of my clinical practice and the fabric that allows me to have a non-judgmental, hopeful, and compassionate presence with those I serve.

Where Was Hope in the Midst of My Despair?

During this period of my life I was naïve and ignorant regarding Church doctrine. It was 1964 and I was only twenty-one. A few years earlier, on January 25, 1959, Pope John XXIII announced he would convene what is commonly known as the Second Vatican Council. The aim of the Council, which was convened on October 11, 1962, and concluded in December of 1965, was to make a shift away from a purely traditionalist perspective to an understanding of the Church in the modern world. The pope hoped that the updating of principles, which was to focus upon pastoral rather than dogmatic issues, would provide a new fabric in which the

Church could stitch new threads of understanding. In so doing, it was hoped that the Church would be brought more in line with the contemporary world and thereby be made more attractive to current parishioners and potential converts. Such shifts would include a movement from exclusiveness to inclusiveness, from severity and condemnation to reconciliation and compassion, from being told what to do to an examination of conscience, from blind acceptance to scholarship, from looking toward eternity to enjoying the fruits of the spirit in the present, and from absolute authority to democratization. As with any major institutional shift, it would take years (into the 1980s) for the Pope's hopes to be realized. This of course would be too late for Rosie and me, though the new fabric of the Church would later warm my heart and provide the material for my eventual spiritual transformation.

> I believe the mystical experience I alluded to when I was an adolescent and the one I had when Rosie and I first fell in love anchored my faith and planted the seed from which my spiritual growth would later blossom.

Even though I became disillusioned with my Church and didn't have a clue about how to extricate myself from my religious quagmire, I couldn't leave Rosie. Since my introduction to the Church's teachings I had been told that faith is a divine gift. I believed this not only intellectually but also in my heart of hearts. In retrospect, I believe the mystical experience I alluded to when I was an adolescent and the one I had when Rosie and I first fell in love anchored my faith and planted the seed from which my spiritual growth would later blossom.

Although I could not stop believing, I didn't know how to believe. I continued to attend Mass but never received communion or went to confession. I did so out of blind obedience and the fear of being further condemned to Hell for committing another mortal sin for not fulfilling my Sunday obligation. Even though I thought of myself as already having been damned, my fallacious way of thinking had me believing I could make matters worse. In Hell there might be different levels of torture and punishment!

Although I attended Mass out of fear, I couldn't help being impressed by the gospel readings and the message they carried. I was moved and enlightened by the stories of the Good Samaritan, the Pharisee and the Tax Collector, and of course the Passion of Christ. They held beautiful messages that resonated within and warmed my heart. They were messages of compassion, altruism, and unconditional love. My heart told me that these stories contained words of wisdom and that they reflected the essence of Christ's teachings. I found myself identifying with and wishing to emulate the loving individuals in the narratives I found inspirational. I wanted to be like the Good Samaritan and kindly and magnanimously care for those in distress. Eventually, this is what I would be called to do. I wanted to be like the pious tax collector and walk in gentleness and humility. I wanted to emulate Jesus and be selfless and forgiving. In the final analysis, the gospel stories confirmed my faith, particularly in my belief that Christ is the Messiah and the Savior of the world.

God often acts in mysterious ways. During this period of my life, he was doing just that. The introduction in John's gospel reads "In the beginning was the Word, and the Word was with God, and the Word was God." I now realize I was listening to God's Word and therefore he was speaking to my soul, which comprehended and embraced his messages. Through the intercession of the Holy Spirit, God was acting as my personal spiritual director. Through the gospel stories, he was laying the foundation for my moral development and spiritual transformation. I also believe that with these stories God was keeping me inside the Catholic Church until, in his own time, I would be reconciled to that Church and live in the fullness of divine love.

Moving Forward—But Not Really

Even though we were unhappy, Richard's birth was like the dawning of a beautiful sunrise, a gift that brought immense joy into our lives. I vividly recall the evening he was born. Rosie awakened me about two o'clock in the morning to tell me she needed to be taken to the hospital. It was raining, so I had to be extra careful driving to Los Angeles's Kaiser Hospital, where Richard was to be delivered. I waited anxiously alone for nearly six hours before he was born. I thanked God when I learned that both he and Rosie were fine. In handing him to me, the nurse first jokingly told me he was a girl and then smiling showed me his penis. After giving him a warm hug and looking at his beautiful face, I proceeded to count all his toes. A short time later, I was allowed to see Rosie (men weren't allowed in the delivery room in those days). She lay quietly, exhausted after having given birth. A spark of warmth glowed in my heart as I handed him over to her.

My feelings of happiness were short-lived. I began to raise more questions about our marriage. Feeling trapped, miserable, and hopeless, I asked Rosie for a separation. I was desperately in need of the time to determine whether or not I truly loved her and, if not, what options we had. I had no one to turn to provide me with support, understanding, and guidance. At least being alone offered me peace and the hope that without the pressure of family life and the constant arguments with Rosie, I could discover the answers to my troubling questions. Did I really love her or did I marry her because she was pregnant and it was the right thing to do? How could I love her if I felt so miserable? If I discovered I didn't love her, would I be committing a mortal sin and be condemned to Hell if we divorced? Was I remaining in the marriage out of obligation? After all, I was the one who took her virginity and she would have the major responsibility for raising Richard if I left. What would my family and friends think if I deserted her? Could I ever overcome the guilty feelings I anticipated I would have if I left? Was I just being selfish? I was a mess, but the one thing I was clear about was that if I remained in the marriage I wanted to do so out of love and not out of guilt, fear, and obligation. I owed that to both Rosie and Richard.

Separating from Rosie was like drawing a breath of fresh air. I could come and go as I pleased and had plenty of solitude to think and reflect on my circumstances. But my respite was short lived. Rosie was very understanding and supportive and, as she has always been, concerned about my well-being. Both our parents and my priest, Father Quinn, were not. Acquiescing to their pressure, I returned home where again felt lost in a quagmire of conflict, confusion, and hopelessness. It took a while to stop wallowing in my misery and move on with my life.

Somehow I managed to compartmentalize my feelings towards my children and my marriage. I felt immense joy when Eileen was born on March 19, 1966. She was a beautiful baby whom we dearly loved and cherished. But afraid that we might feel overwhelmed and burdened with more children, I began using contraceptives. The Church forbade this form of birth control, and I again felt I was in a state of mortal sin and again condemned to Hell. Once more, rather than nourishing my spirit and offering me hope for an enriching life, my Church left me feeling depleted, trapped, lonely, and hopeless.

With the support of Rosie's parents, raising Richard and Eileen was easy, enjoyable, and fulfilling. As parents, Rosie and I were a team, working diligently at shielding them from the unhappiness in our relationship while trying to create a safe and loving home in which they could feel secure and nurtured. We also worked at exposing them to experiences not afforded to us as children, taking them to movies, museums, and on camping trips to national parks across California and the southwest. They were baptized as infants but not raised as Catholics because I didn't wish to burden them with the negative influences I had experienced within the Church.

During this period, Rosie and I worked full time as clerk typists for the city of Los Angeles while I attended Los Angeles City College in the evening four times a week. Our hectic schedules acted as a protective shield. We had little time to argue or be in touch with the depth of our unhappiness. College was very difficult. I was totally unprepared for higher education and struggled for four years just to maintain adequate grades, which only served to reinforce my feelings of inadequacy and stupidity. On the brink of failure, I managed to improve my grade point average enough to transfer to a four year college. This pattern continued in both undergraduate and graduate school: I would dig myself into a hole and then, on the brink of failure, somehow manage to improve my grades. I would eventually fulfill my destiny of receiving a doctoral degree. I now believe the Holy Spirit was present during these times, mysteriously at work, keeping alive my hope of someday finding validation and success in my life.

Chapter 5
My Vocation Finds Me

> Now there are varieties of gifts but the same Spirit; there are varieties of services, but it is the same Lord who activates all of them in everyone.
>
> 1 Corinthians 12:4-6

I struggled to maintain average grades throughout high school, which only served to reinforce my mother's observation that I was stupid, but I was encouraged to go on to college by my teachers, especially by Mr. Lopez. At the time I had no ambitions or idea regarding what profession I would like to pursue. Being forced to declare a major before being admitted into Cal-State Los Angeles, I decided to become a history teacher because history was my favorite subject. Because I continued to struggle academically, attending college was simply hard work and a means to eventually earn a living.

While in my junior year at Cal-State the first of many significant events occurred, events that would continue to unexpectedly redirect my journey and put me on paths for which I had not planned. Erwin McManus writes, "God calls us out of the life we have known and calls us to a life we have never imagined."[1] I can relate to his words of wisdom. While observing my Russian history instructor one day, I suddenly realized that to teach I would have to stand before a classroom of students and be exposed for the fraud I thought I was. I became terrified at the thought, which again put me in touch with my deep feelings of inadequacy and stupidity. In this state of panic, I knew I had to change my major. Because I enjoyed helping people, I decided upon the field of social work. Even though I didn't have any understanding of this profession, I went straight to the registrar's office immediately following class and made the switch.

I didn't realize at the time that we are the sum total of our life experiences and that Holy Spirit uses all those experiences to shape and influence us. Although it is natural to wish to live in consolation and the beauty, joy, and goodness that this world has to offer, it is often through desolation and the experiences of our fears, pains, and sufferings that the Holy Spirit works to transform us into the authentic person we are created to be. As I was to discover later, this was the path on which I was to travel and, through divine grace, the way I was to discover and claim my authenticity.

I did not realize at the time that the Holy Spirit was redirecting me by calling me and putting me on a path of discovery that I would have never imagined. I would eventually use my hidden gifts and talents—gifts and talents that would over time be revealed to me—to serve the well-being of others.

In my first social work class, Dr. Rupp strongly recommended that we students acquire some experience so that we would make an informed decision about entering the profession. Following his suggestion, I immediately turned to the student next to me, Susan Evans, and asked if she knew of a place where I could find such experience. She suggested an agency where she was volunteering, Special Services for Groups, a non-profit private agency specializing in programs to underserved and disenfranchised minority populations in Los Angeles. I took her advice and was accepted as a volunteer to work with a pre-delinquent Mexican-American group whose members were, ironically, attending my old high school. It turned out to be a wonderful experience.

> The Holy Spirit was redirecting me by calling me and putting me on a path of discovery that I would have never imagined. I would eventually use my hidden gifts and talents—gifts and talents that would over time be revealed to me—to serve the well-being of others.

My supervisor, Ellen Dunbar, was an outstanding role model, representing the epitome of what it is to be a professional social worker. She was a person of intelligence, integrity and compassion, a person who had a genuine desire to assist those in need. Besides acquiring the knowledge and skills to work with adolescent groups, I became involved in community organizing and for the first time understood institutional racism and the struggles for justice and equality faced by all ethnic minorities. Armed with this new awareness and my concern for the disenfranchised and underserved, I planned to specialize in community organization upon graduating. I was disappointed to learn from Dr. Rupp that a master's degree in social work was required to take advantage of all the opportunities that profession had to offer.

Barely daring to imagine that I possessed sufficient intelligence for graduate education, after receiving my bachelor's degree

I applied and was accepted into the University of Southern California's Graduate School of Social Work program. Before attending in the fall of 1969, I decided I needed a break from school and worked for a year as a junior probation officer for the County of Los Angeles.

Even my acceptance into USC had little influence on the negative feelings I had about myself. I believed I had been given preferential treatment, that my acceptance had nothing to do with my intelligence but rather was a result of the school's emphasis on affirmative action. I anticipated the worst and assumed that I would fail and be expelled from the program. To my surprise, the reverse happened. Instead of failing, I found myself not only excelling but for the first time actually enjoying school. I attributed this unexpected turn of events to several factors.

First, the pressure from working and going to school was alleviated because I had been awarded a full scholarship and living stipend. Second, I made several friends with whom Rosie and I enjoyed socializing. Third, the professors in the program were personal, supportive, and encouraging. Finally, Norrie Class, a professor for whom I had tremendous respect and admiration, a man of immense integrity and wisdom, took me under his wing and provided me with the guidance and mentoring I required. He began to instill in me for the first time the belief that I wasn't stupid. He also helped me recognize that my difficulties in school had nothing to do with my intelligence but rather with my poor writing skills. As a result, I began receiving tutoring to correct this problem.

While at USC I accepted an invitation by George Nishinaka, Executive Director of Special Services for Groups and a leader in the forefront of the Asian American movement in the United States, to assist in providing leadership to this cause. During this period of American history, Asian Americans were perceived as being a "quiet" minority—self-sufficient and not in need of any social or mental health services. I accepted his invitation and became actively involved in community advocacy, becoming a part of several committees working at the state and national level to dispel the erroneous belief that Asian Americans and Pacific Islanders were not in need of mental health services. The fruits of these efforts are that today, forty years later, Asian Americans and Pacific Islanders are now receiving the full range of mental health, social service, and child welfare services to which they are entitled. It warms my heart when I think that I played a small part in helping this come about.

A Turn in the Road

I enjoyed working directly with clients in my first and second year field work placements at USC but the experiences led me to believe that I wanted to reach and serve more people than working in direct practice would allow. I decided that upon graduation I would accept a position as the director of a non-profit social service agency that provided programs and services to a wide range of individuals in need. Another surprising event would redirect my journey once again and put me on yet another path I had not planned.

My dear friend Tom Carlton and I were working on our master's research paper, "Student and Faculty Perception of Social Work Education." Our project required traveling to graduate social work programs across the country to gather data for our research instrument. Our experience at USC led us to think there might be a significant gap between what students and faculty members believed should be taught in graduate school, how the curriculum should be organized, and how classes should be presented. Our research tested this hypothesis.

The trip itself was a dream come true for me. As an adolescent I had longed to travel across the United States and experience its various landscapes, cultures, and diversity of people. Among the schools we visited were the University of Michigan, the University of Chicago, and the University of Pennsylvania, where we just happened to catch Dr. Joseph Soffen, the person with whom we had the appointment, as he was leaving for the weekend. Had we missed him I would not be where I am today.

Dr. Soffen, the director of the school's doctoral program, was so impressed with our intellectual curiosity and devotion to the field of social work that he encouraged us to apply for entrance into his doctoral program—cost free. I was dumbfounded! Not in my wildest imagination had I envisioned myself pursuing a doctoral degree. We took his advice, applied, and were accepted. I received a no-obligation full scholarship and living stipend for two years from the National Institute of Mental Health (NIMH). Later this award was extended for another year, allowing me to complete my dissertation without the burden of an outside job. With encouragement from my peers, USC faculty members, and Rosie—who had to make the sacrifice of moving away from her very close family, I accepted Penn's invitation.

In the summer of 1971, I graduated with pride with a Master's Degree in Social Work from USC. Later that summer, with about $1,500 in our savings account and all our possession crammed into our 1967 Turquoise Blue Pontiac Bonneville, we set out for Pennsylvania. The next five years would be enriching and growth-producing in ways we never imagined. Rosie found a position she thoroughly enjoyed as a secretary in the Department of Engineering at Penn.

But at the end of my first semester some of my professors were beginning to doubt I had the ability to complete the program. This, according to my faculty advisor, was primarily due to my refusal to speak and engage in class discussions. This made it difficult for my instructors to accurately assess my academic progress. With the support of Rosie, instead of panicking and wallowing in my feelings of stupidity, I demonstrated my scholarship by writing outstanding papers.

To this day I'm not actually sure how I met the challenges of the program. I do remember telling Rosie, and telling myself, that we had sacrificed too much to get where we were. There was no way I was going to be expelled. With the support of the Holy Spirit and my own sense of determination, I rose to the occasion and for the first time, overcame my performance anxiety. Although I remained mute in classes, in the process I relaxed and did what came naturally: to use my analytical and critical thinking skills to express my thoughts, insights, and formulations in my writings and conversations with my professors.

My academic performance put to rest any doubts of those faculty members who questioned my intellectual competence. I moved forward and received my DSW in June of 1974. While receiving my diploma and shaking hands with the dean, I quietly remarked to myself, "Mother, I can't be that stupid." Although I demonstrated at Penn that I could perform well at the highest academic level, it would take several more years for me to fully embrace that thought.

Another Unexpected Turn in the Road

Having received a three-year scholarship from National Institute of Mental Health (NIMH), I felt indebted to the agency and planned to work there after graduation. I was also interested in such work because my involvement in the Asian American movement had allowed me to recognize how changing policy at the national level could positively influence the lives of millions. It was erroneously assumed by many at the time that Asian Americans were seldom in need of social, child welfare, and mental health services and that what few problems we did have were being effectively addressed by the religious groups, family, and social organizations within our communities. I was invited to serve on the first NIMH National Asian American Mental Health Research Board to investigate and dispel these myths. I also served on the first NIMH National Mental Health Asian American Practice and Policy Board to establish policies and programs to serve our neglected and underserved populations.

Although I intended to find employment with NIMH, the Holy Spirit entered my life once again and redirected my journey, putting me on a path I had not planned. A few months before graduating, I received an unexpected call from Dr. Clifford Bodarky, Director of the Department of Mental Health with the Hahnemann Medical School and Hospital in Philadelphia, asking if I would be interested in joining his staff. He had been encouraged to give me a call by Patrick Okura, whom he had met earlier that month at a meeting in Washington. Pat was the representative from NIMH with whom I had been working while serving on various Asian American committees sponsored by his department. He was evidently impressed with my intelligence and skills as a leader and community organizer. And as the cliché goes, Cliff "made me an offer I couldn't refuse."

The popular Outpatient Clinic I was hired to administer served the chronically mentally ill based on a medical model. This approach took mental illness out of the dark ages, when those inflicted with a mental disorder were viewed with superstition. Until the era of modern medicine, individuals with a mental illness were thought of as either being crazy, punished by God, or possessed by demons. However they were viewed, they were to be feared, avoided, and hidden. The mental health movement of the last sixty years has worked diligently towards correcting these misconceptions. Its major objective has been to help the general public recognize that mental illness is a medical problem that can be effectively treated and that, for all intents and purposes, a mentally ill person is no different from the rest of us. Having a mental illness, for example, does not preclude individuals from seeking a loving, fulfilling, and enriching life. But even with today's superior understanding of mental illness, many people still remain ashamed to admit that they themselves or a member of their family suffers from a mental illness or disability.

Learning to Serve Diverse Populations

Our clinic was culturally rich, serving a variety of ethnic groups that included African Americans, Puerto Ricans, Polish, Italians and Chinese. I had a special interest in meeting the needs of those of my own ethnicity and was instrumental in opening an outreach clinic in the middle of Philadelphia's Chinatown.

In addition to serving the chronically mentally ill, the popular clinic also treated a myriad of psychological and interpersonal problems such as poor self-esteem, feelings of loneliness, substance abuse, domestic violence, child abuse, trauma, and marital and family discord. Living in the impoverished area of North Philadelphia, a community immersed in crime, violence, and drug abuse, compounded the difficulties of our clients. Many of them lived well below the poverty line and in housing projects that looked more like prisons than respectable apartments.

Learning to Differentiate Between Temporal and Spiritual Poverty

Working among the poor, deprived, and disenfranchised in North Philadelphia taught me many important lessons about people and life. Significant among them was coming to an understanding of the difference between temporal and spiritual poverty—that living in destitution doesn't necessarily deprive us of our spiritual richness and integrity. This was quite clearly illustrated when I met with a seventy-one year old African American widow living in deprivation in a one bedroom apartment in one of the worst housing projects in North Philadelphia.

Mrs. Hendricks was referred to me by her daughter Janis, who was concerned about her mother's mental and emotional state, living conditions, and the dangers lurking in her immediate surroundings. She felt her mother had become increasingly depressed following the death of her husband, Ted, who had died suddenly from a massive heart attack ten months earlier. She was particularly alarmed over her mother's comments of wishing to be in heaven with her deceased husband of fifty-one years. Unable to convince her mother to accompany her back to her home in Los Angeles, Janis was hoping that, given her mother's depression and what Janis believed to be her suicidal state, we could somehow force Mrs. Hendricks into an assisted living situation.

Mrs. Hendricks gave me a warm welcome into her apartment. It was sparsely furnished and in need of many repairs. After we exchanged pleasantries, she informed me that I needn't worry about her mental condition or the circumstances in which she was living. Listening to her story, it was evident to me that although Mrs. Hendricks was grief stricken at the loss of her beloved husband, she wasn't depressed or suicidal. Though she may have been subsisting on a low fixed income and the external environment in which she lived was colorless, impoverished, and hostile, her interior landscape was vibrant, beautiful and spiritually aglow. Her rich interiority was reflected in her authenticity and spiritual integrity, warm and colorful memories, heartfelt expressions of gratitude, generosity, and hospitality, as well as in her loving and abiding relationship with God. Her mental state was also reflected in her loving and comforting friendships and in the care and devotion of her two children. Mrs. Hendricks lived in blessed simplicity, a simplicity immersed in the wisdom of the heart. Such wisdom intuitively recognizes the reality that love, hope, goodness, and everything else truly meaningful for living a psychological, emotional, and spiritually nourishing life are all found in the course of our ordinary lives no matter in what life circumstances we find ourselves.

> Such wisdom intuitively recognizes the reality that love, hope, goodness, and everything else truly meaningful for living a psychological, emotional, and spiritually nourishing life are all found in the course of our ordinary lives no matter in what life circumstances we find ourselves.

Learning Out of an Empty Cup

There is a popular Zen tale involving a man traveling to Japan seeking knowledge and wisdom from a monk known to be very wise. After exchanging pleasantries the two men sat down to converse. As the visitor began sharing his thoughts and ideas, the hospitable monk began pouring his guest some tea. As the man continued to talk, the monk continued pouring until the tea began spilling over the lip of the cup and pouring onto the table. Still, the man continued talking and the monk continued pouring until his guest, finally realizing what was occurring, excitedly asked the monk what he was doing. The monk gently responded by saying that he could teach the man nothing, because his cup was already too full.

This certainly wasn't my situation when I began my career in clinical practice. My cup was completely empty when I accepted Clifford Bodarky's offer to work for Hahnemann in March of 1974. I didn't have a clue regarding the agency setting, the population I'd be serving, or the services I'd be providing. Although I now feel confident in my therapeutic skills and what I have learned through the years, I have vivid memories of feeling lost, confused, inadequate, and overwhelmed. In the beginning of my career I was also naïve, ignorant, and obviously incompetent. But I took an immediate liking to what I was undertaking and was open and eager to learn and acquire the experience and skills necessary to develop into a competent and helpful therapist. What I didn't recognize at the time was that in letting go of my ego I received the gift of humility. It was a gift that I would later betray, but at the time I was immersed in hopefulness. By embracing my ignorance and lack of experience, I was given the hope that I would become a competent practitioner. At a deeper level, I was beginning to learn that humility is living in a state of gratitude associated with the recognition of the distance between ourselves and God, and an understanding that every blessing we receive from him is pure gift.

My first day at work was a baptism of fire. It began with meeting John Ginyard, the director I was replacing at the popular Outpatient Clinic. During the course of our first transitional meeting, John, who was on emergency duty, received a call from a nurse in the hospital's emergency room. She indicated that some of her staff were trying to calm down a violent, psychotic client who was threatening to, in his own words, "kill every white mother fucker." To my surprise, John informed me that that since I was replacing him, it would be my responsibility to manage this crisis, although he would be by my side.

On the way to the emergency room a few blocks away, John told me he was familiar with the client, Ken, and that the last time he had stopped taking his medication he had provoked a similar incident. He went on to say that during that crisis Ken broke the leg of one of the attendants trying to subdue him. Hearing this tale, like a child in his first adventure leaving home, going to school, and facing the unknown, I began to feel anxious, scared, and helpless. John noticed my fear. Knowing that I had no clinical experience, he provided me words of assurance and reminded me to remain calm and in control of my emotions. He explained that showing any fear or anxiety would only exacerbate Ken's agitated state.

As I entered the emergency room and walked towards the area in which Ken was being detained, I could hear the ruckus he was causing. Before proceeding, I stopped, took several deep breaths, and somehow calmed myself. When I entered the scene it was as the nurse had described. Ken was highly agitated, standing and screaming obscenities while kicking and tossing furniture. The room was in complete disarray. Staff members were standing well out of harm's way trying to verbally settle him down.

For whatever reason, upon seeing me, this 6' 2" emotionally disturbed and confused man immediately calmed down. Looking straight at me, he slowly began to approach, stopping only a few feet away. After a moment of silence his first remark to me was "I love Chinamen, you have some fine women." His comment both caught me by surprise and put me at ease. Somehow in his chaotic and desperate mind he had found a way to feel safe and make a connection. I wasted little time in connecting with him by asking how and why he had come to love Chinese women. Following his explanation, I proceeded with a warm discussion about my family and cultural background. This conversation allowed me to segue into a discussion about my concern for his well-being and the need for him to be hospitalized. After a short while, for reasons I still cannot fathom, he acquiesced and allowed me to walk him to the inpatient unit. Several weeks later, I saw Ken back at our clinic. He was doing fine. The calming effect of his medication had allowed his mind and emotions to rest.

But shortly after my experience with Ken another case reminded me of my ineptitude and how much I still needed to learn. Peggy and Randy, were a very conflicted couple. Each held deep resentments toward the other, took no responsibility for their respective part in contributing to the unhappiness in the marriage, and each felt he or she was the victim in their relationship. It was evident that their hopes and dreams for the marriage hadn't been fulfilled. Instead, their relationship had deteriorated over the years, transforming their feelings of warmth and love into feelings of betrayal, anger, and hostility. During my sessions with them, they could only complain and blame each other for their misery. Caught up in their intensity, antagonism, and negativity, I felt helpless, overwhelmed, and incompetent. For a while I didn't have a clue as to how to proceed. Gathering my wits, I put a stop to the arguing. I then proceeded to point out what was obvious: that they were angry, blaming each other for the problems in the marriage, and exhibiting poor communication skills. I talked about the importance of friendship and respect in a marriage and closed the session with some common sense advice on communicating more effectively. They never returned. I suspect they recognized my fear and incompetence and decided to seek assistance elsewhere. I didn't even have the courage to follow through and ascertain why they hadn't returned.

Learning to Not Make Assumptions

My ineptitude with this case, and the many mistakes I made with others early in my career, impressed upon me how much I needed to learn. Through the process of reading, attending workshops and lectures, participating in training programs, supervision, and consultation, I began to quickly add to my then-empty cup of knowledge and clinical skills. I began learning about, among other things, various theories and assumptions associated with change, motivation, addiction, psychopathology, mental illness, unconscious processes, personality, temperament, and how we think, feel, behave, and communicate. I also began to understand interpersonal relationships, and individual, marital, and family development. The more I learned the more I became interested and excited about learning.

Although my studies and the supervision and training I received at universities were vitally important to the formation of my professional development, equally significant was the acquisition of knowledge and skills I acquired in my clinical experience. This experience included learning from trial and error, learning from what worked in helping clients as well as from what didn't. It also included becoming more mindful of my own feelings and behavior in the session and how they influenced the therapeutic process. It demanded listening to, and learning from, my clients. I began to understand not only how they managed to get into difficulties but also how they managed to overcome them, as well as how they organized their beliefs, feelings, and behaviors to improve the quality of their lives. My experience with Reggie, a nine-year-old, and Barbara, his young, single, African American mother, illustrates this plainly.

Barbara sought assistance at our clinic because of Reggie's failing grades and shy demeanor. Upon meeting him, I discerned that he was a warm, sensitive, reserved, and caring child with at least average intelligence. His reading, writing, and math skills made it evident that his academic problems were not associated with his intellect but were due to a learning disability. After having him tested to determine the extent of his problems, I worked with his mother and school counselor to enroll him in a special education class to assist with his particular disabilities. I also helped Barbara acquire special tutoring for him, for which she was very grateful.

During the course of my work with the family, I observed Reggie being treated very harshly by his mother. Barbara was not only extremely strict but also used corporal punishment to admonish and correct any misbehavior on Reggie's part. Her reprimands appeared to have an intimidating effect, causing him to withdraw into himself. I shared my observations, and along with them my concerns, to Barbara. Although I did not mean to admonish her, Barbara's defensive response told me I must have come across as critical and judgmental. In a firm and assertive voice she told me that I wouldn't be making such comments if I lived in the projects where they lived. She said she couldn't always protect him and that if he didn't learn to be tough and develop a thick skin he wouldn't survive in their neighborhood.

I felt terrible after getting this more complete picture of

her intentions. I recognized that Barbara's strictness was an expression of her love for Reggie and an expression of her fear for his safety and well-being. As she put it, it had to do with his very survival. I apologized for having come across critically. We explored her efforts to protect him and discussed whether those efforts were achieving the results she hoped for. This process led to her recognition that her way of engaging her son was having a negative effect on him and in fact was being counterproductive. We began examining alternatives for helping Reggie to survive, defend himself, and feel safe in his community. The solution we arrived at was, with my support, enrolling him, free of any expense, into a nearby karate class. Also, to help alleviate her fears and improve Reggie's confidence, I worked with Barbara to help him become more assertive.

> I learned firsthand not to make judgments based on outward appearances and behaviors, that I must suspend judgment until I fully understand my clients' reasoning for the way they organized their world.

My experience with Reggie and Barbara taught me lessons that would be woven into the fabric of my clinical practice, lessons that would remain with me throughout my career. I learned firsthand not to make judgments based on outward appearances and behaviors, that I must suspend judgment until I fully understand my clients' reasoning for the way they organized their world. This includes, but is not limited to, their attitudes, values, beliefs, psychological defense mechanisms, available resources, and the culture in which they found themselves immersed.

I learned what now appears obvious, that attitudes and human behavior are strongly influenced and shaped by the cultural and social context in which we are raised, taught, and live and that my own cultural and social context differed greatly from Barbara's. My views and attitudes towards parenting were based on a white middle-class point of view on how children should be raised and treated, while hers were based on a poor, African American perspective. My views and attitudes towards parenting were shaped by living in a safe and resource-rich environment, hers by a dangerous and resource-depleted landscape. My views and attitudes towards parenting were influenced by formal education regarding parenting, while hers were influenced by reality and practicality. I learned that most behavior is reasonable and normal in the context in which a particular person or family lives. To assist my clients, I need to be keenly aware of the circumstances and context in which they lived.

I learned that I must not be judgmental and believe my way of thinking and behaving superior to that of my clients, that I must understand and respect our differences, and that I needed to work diligently to keep my personal biases out of the therapeutic process. I also learned that to be helpful I must be client-centered rather than centered on my own ideas or some abstract model of practice or the practical mandates of the setting in which I am working. I learned that to effectively assist those I serve I must honor the clinical axiom of starting where the client is—that the starting point in the therapeutic process is my client's reference point and not mine. What's more, I learned that to be useful I must engage in a collaborative process with my clients, recognizing that their ideas, beliefs, and experiences should be central to an effective treatment plan,

Working with Reggie and his mother, I learned to admit rather than hide or ignore my mistakes. Had I not acknowledged my slip-up in inadvertently being accusatory and judgmental, Barbara would have remained unable to respect or trust me. I suspect this would have led to her being resistant to any of my attempts to help. Implicit in my acknowledging and apologizing for my blunder was the important message that I respected and was genuinely concerned about her and Reggie's well-being. I created a bridge upon which we could travel to find a solution to her distress.

Learning from Experts

Taking a position at Hahnemann as director of a small outpatient community mental health clinic launched me on a professional career I couldn't have imagined. I was exposed to a wide range of specialties in the mental health field, like intensive psychotherapy, dance therapy, sex therapy, play therapy, and marital and family therapy. Equally significant, I was fortunate in receiving training from world-renowned leaders and pioneers in family therapy. I will forever be indebted to these men and women for not only sharing their skills, knowledge, and wisdom with me but also for providing me the support, understanding, and validation that allowed me to acquire a confidence in myself that had eluded me my whole life.

My initial training came under the tutelage of Dr. Ed Volkman, the clinic's medical director, who later became a dear friend and role model. He was an excellent supervisor, teacher, and administrator, an exceptional clinician, and a passionate and dedicated professional. I admired his integrity, sensitivity, and genuine concern for his clients. I wanted so much to emulate him that at times I even found myself mimicking some of his gestures. Only later, as a therapist, did I come to understand that admiring the qualities of another person is also an affirmation of ourselves—that those qualities we admire in others exist in us and are only waiting to be discovered and expressed.

> Admiring the qualities of another person is also an affirmation of ourselves. Those qualities we admire in others exist in us and are only waiting to be discovered and expressed.

Ed was an expert in intensive psychotherapy that is rooted in psychodynamic theory and its application in working with individuals, couples, and families. Simply put, this model emphasized intrapsychic and unconscious processes and how they influenced personal growth and development and interpersonal relationships. Clients were perceived as being insecure, emotionally weak, and having deficits that needed rectifying, but according to this approach, these insecurities stemmed from unresolved issues with their parents or caretakers. If, for example, children were made to feel ugly, inferior, and unlovable, they would carry these feelings and distorted perceptions into their adult lives, inhibiting them from developing enriching and fulfilling lives. Or if children were raised in an environment in which they were abandoned, abused, and discounted, as adults they might either avoid entering a relationship for fear of this reoccurring or, once in a relationship, project such thoughts and feelings on to their partner.

In practice, this model emphasized a hierarchal relationship between therapists and their clients, with therapists being the expert in the relationship. We were expected to be responsible for diagnosing problems presented and treating them with various therapeutic interventions. The primary objective of therapy was to help clients recognize the etiology—the ultimate root—of their problems, overcome fears and insecurities, and make prudent decisions and choices that enriched rather than diminished their lives. To be effective in achieving therapeutic goals, we were also expected to be respectful and supportive while maintaining a professional distance by treating clients with a "kind indifference."

Under Ed's supervision my hope of achieving competence as a therapist was realized. With his guidance, I grew knowledgeable in psychodynamic theory, psychopathology, and the use of intensive psychotherapy to treat clients. I also learned to be comfortable with the use of silence, challenging my clients, and being aware of not imposing or transferring my insecurities onto my clients. In addition I became familiar with the use of medication in treating the various mental disorders such as schizophrenia and major depression. What I learned most from Ed was something that changed my perspective towards the mentally ill and clients in general. It would play a major role in my clinical practice throughout my career. He taught me to separate the person from his or her problem. I came to understand that people are not defined by their problems or mental illness.

Put another way, people may have a problem or mental illness but are not themselves the problem. A client is not his or her mental illness. For example, an individual with a diagnosis of schizophrenia should not be labeled a "schizophrenic," as though the illness he or she inherited defined the essence of his or her nature. Labeling people was a widely-held attitude at the time, pervasive even among mental health professionals. Ed taught me instead to look at and treat behavioral problems brought to our attention as symptoms of something deeper, while recognizing and treating with respect the integrity of all those exhibiting them.

What impressed me the most about the additional training I received at Hahnemann was the respect the experts in these special areas of practice held for one another. They weren't competitive but rather cooperative, collaborative, appreciative of one another's expertise, and open to learning from one another. For a novice like me, it was a rich educational landscape in which to be immersed. I took from this experience an appreciation and respect for the various ways we professionals could help those in need of our assistance. It also planted the seeds for me to later grow into an eclectic practitioner, having the ability to blend a variety of therapeutic modalities to meet the unique needs and circumstances of the individuals, couples, and families I served.

During my tenure at Hahnemann an unexpected thing happened that would have a profound impact on the development of my career. I met and received training from two of the profession's foremost leaders in family therapy, Jay Haley, founder of Strategic Therapy, and Salvador Minuchin, creator of Structural Family Therapy. Both men were brilliant, dedicated to their profession, and pioneers in their field. My training with them led me to a major paradigm shift in my practice. Instead of seeing my clients' problems as lying

> Instead of seeing my clients' problems as lying only within the individual, I could also see how they are a manifestation of a dysfunctional family system.

only within the individual, I could also see how they are a manifestation of a dysfunctional family system. In Jay's view, peoples' problems lay within the manner in which individuals attempted to communicate. Sal saw how families did or did not maintain appropriate boundaries within their various sub-groups such as siblings, couples, and parent-child. Both saw that problems were not just associated with the past but with how individuals were functioning in the present.

Jay was not a therapist but masterful planner and strategist who led me to understand communication theory, one of the primary means for assessing, comprehending, and diagnosing family functioning. Among other things, I learned that communication often has a history. I recall, for example, a husband exploding at his wife when she made a comment regarding his lack of sensitivity. Until I explored and discovered the reason for his angry response towards an apparently innocent comment, I thought he was being unreasonable and overreacting to her remark. During that exploration I discovered that her comment had a history and that for years she had used that very comment to criticize and express anger about his perceived lack of concern for her well-being. Her comment had a history and was like a fuse on a stick of dynamite just waiting to be detonated.

From Jay I also learned that all behavior is communication and inherent in any communication are multiple, often conflicting, messages. A mother, for example, may verbally express love toward her son, but her critical and indifferent behavior conveys the opposite. Under Jay's tutelage, I learned to track communication patterns and to reframe or reinterpret what appeared to be negative messages into positive ones. In many instances, all that was required in helping clients was to assist them in making just one major affective, behavioral, or perceptual shift. If, for example, a wife came into therapy feeling unloved but left feeling loved, her attitude toward her husband would shift from being negative to positive. If a husband came into therapy being verbally abusive but left never again behaving in such a manner, his wife could begin to alleviate her fears of being verbally attacked. If a wife came into therapy not believing the sincerity of her husband's words of endearment but left believing them, she could begin once again to feel the warmth of his love.

I learned that by correcting painful, dysfunctional, and disruptive communication patterns through the use of strategic and powerful interventions, clients could make immediate and profound changes. I learned to give homework assignments to facilitate and reinforce the changes created in the sessions. Finally, in a climate in which our clients were generally held responsible for failed interventions or lack of success in treatment, I learned from Jay that the major responsibility for a positive outcome in treatment lay with the therapist, not with our clients. If therapeutic interventions failed, it was in all likelihood due to our incompetence, lack of skill, or poor judgment.

Unlike Jay, Sal was himself a therapist. Observing him working with families was like watching a brilliant conductor leading a symphony orchestra. I would watch in awe as he effortlessly, skillfully, and creatively engaged and helped those he served. His effectiveness, gift for quickly conceptualizing issues, and ability to draw upon a seemingly endless history of successful interventions was amazing and inspiring, instilling in me the hope that someday I could come close to his level of proficiency and expertise.

Under Sal's supervision, we were encouraged to experiment, use our imagination, and be creative. I learned to be imaginative, flexible, and adaptable in using his model. In the process, I acquired a host of therapeutic interventions upon which to draw. I recall, for example, an adolescent who had difficulty expressing his angry and hurt feelings. I had him sit on a red chair and express to his mother what it felt like being on the hot seat. In addition to having the ability to select from a variety of therapeutic tools, continuing to add to my repertoire of interventions has allowed me to redirect my efforts when what I first attempt is ineffective.

Among all the useful lessons I learned from Sal, the most important was the recognition that once I joined and connected with a family, I temporarily became one of its members, influencing and being influenced by them. To be effective I needed to join with them in a manner that cultivated harmony and synchronicity. In so doing, respect could be earned, trust established, and the collaboration critical to success achieved.

The training I received from Jay and Sal at the Philadelphia Child Guidance Clinic was outstanding. Unlike my previous experience, I received live supervision. They observed my sessions from behind a two-way mirror, and when I was not being helpful they called me out of the room to provide instructions on how to proceed in a manner that was more useful. I recall, for example, being observed by Sal while working with a middle-aged, single African American mother, Ms. Brown, who sought help for her two children, Cliff, age nine, and Caroline, age thirteen. I remember being stiff, reserved, and analytical while interviewing the mother. I was following the script for which I had been trained at Hahnemann—that of being kind but objective while following a prescribed template. My intent was to obtain a clear and comprehensive developmental history on each of the children. After a few minutes, Sal called me out of the session and instructed me to relax, stop asking questions as though I was following a script from a manual, and join in the conversation with the family. Following his instructions had an immediate impact. Everyone relaxed, became more animated, and spoke more openly. Being relaxed and connected with them allowed me to conduct the interview in a leisurely and fluid manner. This experience taught me the importance of first establishing a warm and safe atmosphere for my clients before delving into their presenting concerns.

Sal also taught me the importance of acting naturally and authentically in sessions. With this in mind and with his encouragement to follow my intuition, be spontaneous, and use my imagination, I devised a creative intervention that I would use in the next session with the Brown family. A few minutes into the interview, my intuition told me that beneath the angry and critical comments Ms. Brown was directing toward Caroline were deep feelings of worry and concern. Instead of focusing on her complaints and launching the intervention I had planned on, I listened to my instincts and drew attention to what I believed to be her underlying feelings.

My instincts were correct. Ms. Brown began to cry. She shared her deep concerns for her daughter and her fear that she wouldn't be able to shelter and protect her from the negative influences and destructive forces that permeated their community. I immediately recognized that what Ms. Brown needed above all was emotional support, comfort, and encouragement, which I was uniquely positioned to provide.

Learning to Feel Competent

What I learned from Ed, Jay, and Sal was invaluable, and over time it led to my growing feeling of competence. My development is well-illustrated by my experience with another polarized couple, Christy and Mel. Like Peggy and Randy, they came to therapy feeling extremely angry and resentful toward each other. Neither was interested in what the other was feeling or what the other had to say. Both felt disrespected, unheard, and discounted, and each felt that he or she was the only victim in the relationship. Neither would accept responsibility for the unhappiness they were experiencing. During the course of the first session, Mel became enraged when he felt criticized, verbally attacking Christy with a barrage of condescending remarks. I immediately intervened and de-escalated the hostility by preventing any further interaction. But unlike with Peggy and Randy, I didn't feel overwhelmed, insecure, and helpless. Instead I felt I had an accurate assessment regarding the factors that contributed to their distress, factors that remained hidden from their view.

After preventing Christy and Mel from arguing and expressing their hostile feelings, I shared my clinical observations. I helped them to recognize their differences in communication styles, underlying vulnerabilities, and the effects of outside influences on their relationship, particularly the intrusion of Christy's family. Taking what I had learned from Jay and Sal, now understanding that words and feelings conveyed multiple messages, I reframed Mel's angry outburst with a positive connotation. I did this by sharing with Mel my belief that his anger not only represented his feeling criticized but also his feeling misunderstood and, at a deeper level, unloved. After pausing and giving my comments some thought, he agreed. Believing he felt supported and understood by me, I then asked him to share those feeling with Christy.

But before having Mel proceed, I asked Christy to just listen and not respond to his comments. I did this knowing that she was still feeling upset from Mel's criticism and therefore in all probability would be unable to embrace his change in demeanor and gentle words. I would need to prepare her to receive his message. I also wanted to maintain balance in the session by letting Christy know that I could also recognize and empathize with her deeper thoughts and feelings. Furthermore, I wanted Mel to hear what might be behind his wife's hurt feelings. I was able to accomplish these objectives by sharing with Christy that I suspected she felt the same way as her husband, that she too felt misunderstood and, at a deeper level, unloved. She immediately agreed with this statement. I then shared with both of them that it was sad that they had lost the loving feelings that had initially brought them together. I then proceeded by asking them not to speak but to sit quietly and reflect on what I had just conveyed. The purpose of this intervention was to foster an atmosphere of sadness and maybe even love rather than hostility.

When it was evident that the couple had softened, I began assisting them in focusing upon and recognizing the positive attributes in their marriage and each other. Knowing that the relationship was still fragile and that any further conflict would resurrect hurtful and angry feelings, I shared my thoughts as to why I believed they needed time to disengage emotionally. I suggested homework. First, to prevent any further disruption and hurt feelings, they were not to discuss any of the issues that brought them to therapy. These would be addressed in therapy in later sessions. Second, I suggested that they go on a date and work at having a relaxing time. This suggestion was aimed at helping them to once again be comfortable in each other's presence. Third, I suggested that they list twenty to twenty-five things that they loved, admired, or respected in their spouse. They were not to share this information but simply reflect on what they had written. Their thoughts would be discussed later in therapy. The purpose of this assignment was to put them in touch with the positive things that had brought them together in the first place. Next, they were to write five things they hoped for and wanted from their marriage.

My purpose in these assignments to Christy and Mel was to focus them on the future and set the stage for their participation in a solution-oriented therapeutic process, a process that would minimize the occurrence of hurtful and painful feelings. Finally, I asked them to each list five things that they could do to improve the relationship. They were not to share this information with their spouse at any time but to hold themselves accountable to that which they had written. To help insure their follow through, I asked them to share this information with me. The purpose of this suggestion was to help them take individual responsibility for moving the relationship in a positive direction.

Clinical interventions are a process of trial and error. In this instance my interventions and suggestions led to a dramatic change in the couple's attitude and demeanor. The two returned the following week in a positive, friendly, and hopeful frame of mind. Although many of their disturbing issues and hurt feelings remained, that didn't prevent them from collaborating with me in finding solutions to their problems and beginning to lay them to rest.

The training I received in Philadelphia provided the foundation for the transformation of my clinical expertise into what I can only describe as an art form. To paraphrase Sal, being a therapist is like being a pianist who in the beginning is a novice and separated from the piano but after years of tutoring, practicing, and performing eventually evolves into an artist and becomes one with the instrument. In the mental health profession, we begin as novices, working at developing our skills and doing the best we can to help our clients. But with years of excellent training, supervision, and practice, we hope to become an artist, one with the therapy that we practice.

Watching Sal work evoked strong feelings of admiration in me I recognized to be, in actuality, self-confirmation. This strengthened my understanding that there is a natural affinity between our own abilities and the qualities we admire in others. Sal elicited within me the hope that I could one day acquire the level

> I unknowingly moved from seeing social work as my default profession, merely my job, to seeing it as work I fully and sincerely embraced.

of proficiency and creativity he possessed. In the process of working under his tutelage, I unknowingly moved from seeing social work as my default profession, merely my job, to seeing it as work I fully and sincerely embraced. I began to find fulfillment and enjoyment not only in clinical practice but in all the roles I filled within its domain. Being enriched by my experiences, with the guidance of the Holy Spirit, my profession began to evolve into my vocation. I would have to overcome several major challenges before this came to pass completely, but, I would eventually fulfill my destiny by growing into the person God designed me to be. Of this I have no doubt.

Reconciliation

Another renowned expert and pioneer in the field of family therapy in which I had the privileged of being trained was Dr. Ivan Boszormenyi-Nagy, the founder of Contextual Family Therapy. His was a multidimensional model whose major focal point was on the importance of family loyalty. Unlike Jay and Sal, he took into consideration both inter-personal and intra-psychic dynamics. Also, unlike them, with their focus on the present, Nagy focused on the past. He emphasized laying to rest unresolved past conflicts with members of the client's family that interfered with his or her ability to establish nurturing, caring, and supportive current relationships. I learned from him how negative patterns can be passed from one generation to another and how disloyalty to family can cause feelings of guilt, shame, and regret. I learned how to help family members free themselves from the past.

Nagy believed that to be proficient with his model, we therapists need, if necessary, to go through the experience of finding peace with those in our own family with whom we had unresolved issues. After months of his tutelage and with his encouragement, support, and guidance, I returned home to make peace with my parents, particularly with my mother. It took all the courage I could muster to stand before them alone, to acknowledge their support and the sacrifices they made so that I could have the opportunity to live a happy and meaningful life. I gave them credit for my academic achievements and my current success. I closed my conversation by asking their forgiveness for the trouble I had caused. I'm not sure if my parents fully comprehended what I was attempting to convey, but they nodded their approval. And from that day forward, my mother treated me with respect. I learned later from my sister Liz that my father took pride in telling his friends about my success and accomplishments. For me, I felt I had matured into an adult and that a tremendous emotional burden had been lifted from my heart. With this liberation, I felt open to experiencing and seeing my parents in a different light. I now lived in the hope that things could continue to improve between me and my parents, and they did.

An Unexpected Discovery

Another unexpected but important event during this period would have a major influence on my career. The administrators at Hahnemann supported my training by paying my tuition and giving me the time to attend the weekly sessions. In return, I agreed to pass on what I learned by offering to our staff a series of workshops. Upon receiving my certificate of completion from the Child Guidance Clinic, I spent a month preparing for my first presentation. Having never conducted a workshop, lacking any confidence in my ability to communicate before an audience, and still carrying my mother's message that I was stupid, I felt extremely insecure and worried regarding what I was about to undertake.

My presentation turned into a transforming experience. Inexplicably, I got in touch with a side of me that I didn't know existed. It turned out I am a natural and gifted presenter. I discovered I am articulate, can easily connect with members of an audience, and have no problems addressing their questions. From my opening remarks in my first workshop onward, I felt confident, relaxed, and engaging. I found myself drawing from different clinical experiences to make the workshop lively, informative, and interesting. The feedback from the workshop evaluations indicated that I had done an outstanding job and that the participants felt the subject was presented in a clear, thorough, and comprehensive manner. Adding to the enrichment of my grateful heart, I was completely taken aback when I was told by some individuals that it was the best workshop they had ever attended. But even with this positive feedback it took me years to fully embrace my newfound gifts and talents.

During this time at the Child Guidance Clinic, I received an unexpected gift from Sal. He told me that I had conducted a superb session and that he couldn't teach me anything more. I couldn't refute his comments because I held him in such high regard. He was the expert. If he said I was ready, he had to be right. Sal's validation was a wonderful gift, helping to further erase my mother's demeaning words, still imprinted in my heart, that I was stupid. He evidently saw things in me that were below the surface of my awareness. Because I hadn't yet evolved as a therapist, I didn't have a place to hold his compliments. Years later, when I began formulating my conceptualization for being a spiritually based practitioner I recognized and comprehended what Sal so astutely observed so many years ago. Validation is the best gift we have to give, and it costs us nothing.

I also had the privilege of knowing and working with Reverend Hoe, an elderly wise man respected and admired by the entire Chinese community. He was a saintly person who worked tirelessly to nurture and guide his flock while doing everything he could to improve the social, economic, and living conditions in his community. Without his support and guidance, I couldn't have completed my dissertation, which focused on the efficacy of the social service agencies in Philadelphia's Chinatown, or worked successfully toward opening the first outreach mental health facility in that community.

Reverend Hoe, with his wisdom, kindness, and compassionate heart, graced the lives of countless individuals, including me. I will never forget the day when he shared with me his belief that I was "a wise young man." His comments brought tears to my eyes. Though I couldn't fully embrace his observation at the time, I couldn't deny it either. To do so would insult his intelligence and good judgment. Today I carry his words as a sacred gift, one that I treasure and keep in the depths of my heart.

A Journey of Hope

Later I came to recognize and appreciate more fully the influence both Reverend Hoe and Sal had on my life. Not only did I begin to inhabit the landscape in which they traveled. They unknowingly introduced me to the mystery, the "not yet" dimensions inherent in hope. They saw in me part of my divine substance, that aspect of me that is inherently directed at attending to the well-being of others. For Sal, it was the grace of my capacity to look into the hearts of my clients and see the essence of those I served with warmth and compassion. For Reverend Hoe it was my gifts of prudence and wisdom. Although I already possessed these attributes, they lived mainly beyond my conscience awareness, waiting to be discovered. They rested in the mystical state of "not yet" and in this realm waited for the intercession of the Holy Spirit to be revealed, comprehended, and embraced. Together, these wonderful men provided me with two pillars that would serve as the foundation for my eventual spiritual transformation

Since the beginning of my professional career in Philadelphia, my experiences with those I served shaped and continue to reshape and transform my attitudes, perceptions, and feelings toward not only clinical practice but also my philosophy of life. I now recognize that the work I do with others is reciprocal, that I am engaged in a collaborative process in which I am inherently both giving and receiving. I have come to learn that my clients are also my teachers, teaching me about the beauty inherent in everyone, teaching me about honor, courage, fidelity, commitment, love, and—most importantly—teaching me about the Divine Presence working in our lives. I have

> I now recognize that the work I do with others is reciprocal, that I am engaged in a collaborative process in which I am inherently both giving and receiving. My clients are also my teachers.

also come to learn that as therapists we are in a privileged position because those we serve, many of whom are in a state of despair or at a crossroads in their lives, trust us with their well-being—some with their very survival. They hope we can support and guide them through their confusion, pain, suffering, and tragedies. They also hope we can help them lay to rest the fears that prevent them from living loving and satisfying lives or finding meaning and acceptance in personal tragedies and significant losses. Finally, I have come to learn that I am in the business of pain, suffering, despair, love, healing, and hope.

I have also come to learn that my professional development was not only a journey in the acquisition of knowledge and skills in offering hope to those I served, it was also a journey of hope for me. The process of acquiring clinical competency, the affirmation I received from clients, the discovery of my gifts as a trainer, and the validation that I received from mentors infused in me the hope that I could eventually overcome and heal from the deep feelings of shame, worthlessness, and stupidity that disturbed me throughout my life. In the process of fostering healing among others, I was being healed myself. In the process of offering hope to those I served, the Holy Spirit was offering me that same gift.

Chapter 6
Gift of Freedom

Transcendence

My Mind trembles with the shimmering leaves.
My heart sings with the touch of sunlight.
My life is glad to be floating with all things
Into the blue of space and dark of time.

RABINDRANATH TAGORE[1]

 My experiences in Philadelphia not only put me on the path of psychological and emotional freedom, but offered me the hope of religious freedom as well. This grace was given to me after having accepted an invitation from two close friends, Marie and Jim, to attend services with them at the Daylesford Abbey, a small progressive Catholic community located in Paoli, Pennsylvania. The emphasis in this community of Norbertine Fathers was on warmth, acceptance, personal responsibility, and religious freedom. This emphasis was reflected in their greetings, social interactions, warmth of expressions, homilies, and the joyful, loving, and festive manner in which Mass was celebrated. I had never experienced this caring and spiritual dimension of the Church.

I felt so safe and enriched by the loving atmosphere of the Abbey that before leaving I spoke with one of the priests regarding the incident in which another priest had told me I must leave Rosie and about my feelings of being damned for practicing birth control. The monk spoke with me regarding the notion of free will and personal responsibility, that among other things, sin was a matter of conscience. I learned that a basic tenet of the Church is that our individual conscience is inviolable and that even if our conscience is in error according to official Church teachings it must be followed. That being said, Catholics are required to inform our conscience of the Church's teachings to the greatest extent possible. But formation of conscience also involves input from our intellect as well as what is called the "magisterium"— the authoritative teachings of the Church. Physical and social sciences, the priest said, and our own life experience also serve to inform and form our conscience. I took his consultation to mean that God would judge me on what I truly believed in my heart was the right and loving thing to do and not on anyone else's opinion on the matter I was examining, not a priest in the confessional or the Pope himself.

This priest's consultation gave me permission to enter into what he called "a process of discernment," which allowed me to examine my conscience and judge what I believed to be spiritually true. This process included prayer and the involvement of the Holy Spirit in examining the issue at hand. In this instance, it was a question of whether or not I believed that the Church's ban on the use of contraceptives as a means of birth control under the circumstances at that time in my life was a mortal sin. I recognized that it was important that I enter this process with openness, sincerity, and honesty; otherwise I would simply be making a decision that was convenient in rationalizing my self-serving needs.

Through this discernment process the following logic led me to believe that it was not a sin for me to continue practicing birth control. First, I believed that my lovemaking with Rosie was just that, "making love." It was a beautiful expression of our marital relationship, uniting our minds, body, emotions, and spirits in an intimate, loving, and holy union. It was also a fulfillment of the promise that was offered in God's blessing of our marriage, for it was truly "the uniting of two into one." For me, such an act was entered into for its own sake and did not necessarily have to lead to having children. It seems to me that if the purpose of lovemaking is simply to procreate, perhaps with the by-product of having pleasure, then marital sex would be a functional rather than blessed experience.

Second, the Church in fact offered a type of birth control, what it termed the "rhythm or natural method." Although the Church presents moral justification for this approach, its intent is to help a couple plan if and when to have children. For me, it doesn't make a difference what method—"natural" or not—is used to meet this end. Furthermore, after reading and examining the Church's position, I am left with the belief it wasn't as "natural" an approach as we are led to believe. Instead of allowing sex between a married couple to be flexible, adaptive, and spontaneous, the "natural family planning" system seems to me structured, planned, and calculating.

Having discerned what I believed to be true regarding the use of contraceptives, I no longer felt I was condemned to Hell. I had been released from the despairing feelings I had been carrying for the years. Furthermore, a major barrier had been removed between me and my participation in the Church. Each time I celebrated Mass at the Daylesord Abbey, I left feeling spiritually enriched and nourished. And though there had been a shift in my feelings during Mass and another seed for my spiritual formation and transformation had been planted, my faith in and relationship with God and the Church had not been fundamentally altered. That would come fourteen years later.

Chipping Away at the Invisible Barrier

I would characterize the time we lived in Philadelphia as being up to then the happiest and most hopeful of my life. Professionally, I couldn't have been more satisfied, having received training and supervision from experts I admired and wished to emulate. With their guidance, I had grown from a novice into a competent therapeutic practitioner. I was also blessed with discovering that I had a hidden talent, that of being an excellent instructor. Psychologically, I had graduated with a doctoral degree and thus began removing the myth told to me by my mother that I was stupid. The validation I received from Sal and Reverend Hoe played a major role in helping me to accept that I was a worthwhile person. Finally, laying to rest the conflict that had divided me from my parents my entire life also helped me make major strides toward removing some of my major personal psychological insecurities.

Moving to Philadelphia was also the best thing that could have happened for our marriage. For the first time Rosie and I became self-reliant. We made friends, worked together on my school projects, and traveled as a family extensively throughout the East Coast. We also took advantage of the many cultural activities offered in Philadelphia and nearby Manhattan. Most memorable was my role in organizing the first Asian American organization in Philadelphia, the Asian American Council, and being instrumental in helping to save Philadelphia's Chinatown from the ravages of urban renewal. All these rich experiences began chipping away at the invisible barrier I had erected between Rosie and me, allowing us to recapture some of the warm, caring, and loving feelings that prevailed in our youth.

Among all the wonderful things that happened to us while living in the East was witnessing the changing of the seasons. The first time we experienced New England in the fall, our family was overwhelmed with the beauty that unfolded before us. Every year thereafter, we'd take trips into the countryside to immerse ourselves into this miracle of nature, in the crisp fresh air that reigned, the lavish green grass that blanketed the ground, and the kaleidoscope of spectacular colors of the leaves that adorned the surrounding trees. Like nature's seasons, my interior season also changed. Since being told by the priest to leave Rosie, my heart had been immersed in a landscape of blacks and grays. With the many blessings I was receiving, that landscape transformed into one of bright and lovely colors, the colors of love, peace, friendship, success, community, and—as always—hope.

Homecoming

Although we found living in Philadelphia satisfying and rewarding, Rosie was very homesick. After making two failed bids to buy a home near Philadelphia, in the summer of 1976 we decided to return to Los Angeles. I began my search for a leadership position in the field of mental health. Sam Taylor, a former professor to whom I turned for assistance, told me of an opening as executive director of the Family Service Association of Riverside, a small non-profit United Way agency located in a city just sixty miles east of Los Angeles. I contacted Festus Webley, a former classmate at USC who was on the agency's board of directors, regarding the position. He explained that the agency was part of the family service movement and one of several hundred such agencies serving cities, counties, and provinces across the United States and Canada. He also explained that the Family Service Association had been financially mismanaged recently, putting its solvency in jeopardy. The former director had also alienated the organization from the other mental health, social service, and United Way agencies in the community. But Festus' description of the agency's mission, programs, and problems led me to believe that it might be the ideal place for me. I could use the many skills I had acquired during the past few years to assist in re-establishing its former well-respected status. I applied and was hired for the position. Once again the Holy Spirit had redirected my journey. Instead of living and working in Los Angeles, as I had anticipated, I was now in Riverside, which turned out to be much better for us for many reasons.

Our initial plan had been to remain in Riverside only until I returned the agency to its former stature. We then hoped to find a way to move closer to our families. Instead, we quickly became acclimated to our new situation and the advantages it afforded. The cost of living was far lower than in Los Angeles. Housing was affordable, our children could walk to school, and everything, including my office, was in close proximity to our home. We didn't have rush hours to contend with and had easy access to the nearby mountains, desert, and ocean, which we visited frequently. Rosie found a clerical position with Riverside Junior College that she thoroughly enjoyed. We developed a sense of community and felt we had a voice in its affairs. Finally, our frequent weekend drives into Los Angeles to visit our extended families took just an hour.

The Expert

I thoroughly enjoyed my new position and over time helped the agency to regain its stellar reputation. In the process, I rose to a position of leadership among other United Way and family service agency directors. In my efforts to promote marital and family therapy in the region and even, through the Western Region of Family Service Associations of America, into parts of Canada, I gained a reputation as an expert in this area of clinical practice. I was invited to give workshops by departments of mental health, family and social services agencies, and child welfare organizations throughout the southwestern United States. I was also invited to teach as an adjunct professor in Loma Linda University's Graduate Department of Marital and Family Therapy and at USC's Graduate School of Social Work. With this experience of teaching, training, supervising, and consulting—and beginning to recognize the knowledge and skills I acquired from these undertakings—I gradually came to embrace my new status in the field of social work.

Freedom from My Self-Imposed Muteness

You might think that with all the teaching and training I had undertaken my feelings of shame and inadequacy at asking questions or making comments in workshops I attended would have diminished, but the damaging effects of my childhood traumas wouldn't stop this intense shyness from recurring over and over again. This finally changed during a workshop I attended given by two world-renowned family therapists, Fred and Bunny Duhl.

Years later I was to learn that once a person is genuinely ready to challenge his or her worst fears, the opportunity to do so arises. I have worked with many clients to help them reach this point in their therapy. I also learned that many clients, simply by seeking therapy, have already made the internal decision to change their circumstances. They are already prepared to challenge the obstacles or relationships that have kept them in a psychological, emotional, or interpersonal prison. Why some of us can reach such a point while others cannot remains a puzzle to me.

> Many clients, simply by seeking therapy, have already made the internal decision to change their circumstances. They are already prepared to challenge the obstacles or relationships that have kept them in a psychological, emotional, or interpersonal prison.

In my case, I was ready to challenge my fear of being made to feel embarrassed or ashamed. I was ready to reclaim my voice. Fred and Bunny Duhl provided me with that opportunity. During their presentation, I felt they weren't being clear on several points. Unwilling to remain in my self-imposed muteness, for the first time since being publically humiliated by Ms. Jean Beauvoir in the eighth grade, I overcame my fear of exposure and in the midst of an audience, asked for a point of clarification. As I raised my hand the tension in my neck, back, and shoulders was so severe I almost fainted, but somehow I managed to make myself clear. My self-imposed muteness came to an abrupt end. This corrective experience silenced once and for all my mother's repeated assertion that I was stupid.

My questions were well received and the speakers' responses helped to clarify issues I believe others were finding confusing as well. But even if my comments had been dismissed and the Duhls had become defensive or antagonistic, I believe I would not have withdrawn again into my uncommunicativeness. It has been my experience that once individuals have found the fortitude to challenge that which has kept them emotionally paralyzed, they never retreat. This is due, in part, to the fact that it is not the outcome of the encounter that is important. More often than not it doesn't really matter what happens following the challenge. What is critical is that the individuals have somehow found the strength, courage, and determination to honor themselves and, in so doing, set themselves free of their worst fears.

Freedom from My Mother's Criticism

Shortly before I left my job at the Family Services Association of Riverside, in April of 1984, my mother passed away from a stroke. She was seventy-three years old. It was a devastating moment for my father, her loving and devoted companion for over fifty years. I was saddened as well to hear the news of her death. Since we had managed to reconcile our differences ten years earlier, my mother had begun to treat me with due respect. This allowed me to see her in positive rather than negative light and to finally feel comfortable in her presence. My sadness and feelings of endearment were reflections of the loss of a loving relationship between mother and son that might have been but never was.

While making my mother's funeral arrangements, my father did something quite remarkable for me. He instructed Mr.

Quan, the person in charge, to give me the honor of giving my mother's eulogy. Mr. Quan was shocked by the instruction. It was unheard of in Chinese culture for a child to give his parent's eulogy. Making it even more astonishing, I was not even the oldest son but the youngest. My father's request brought tears to my eyes, because I knew he was showing me respect by making me his spokesperson and giving me a new place in our family, a place of honor.

In preparing for her eulogy, I wanted to give a heartfelt and sincere remembrance of my mother's life, one that would honor her and my father. I spoke with my siblings, aunts and uncles, and some of her friends to gather material that I could incorporate into her story. What I learned was enlightening. My major discovery was that, because of near-death experiences while giving birth to some of my siblings, she was terrified of childbearing. She didn't wish to continue having children but reluctantly acquiesced to my father's desire for a large family. This discovery gave me a partial understanding of why she may have been unable to love and connect with me.

In learning these things about my mother, I began seeing her story in a much broader context, a context that included her relationship with her friends, culture, and—most importantly—with my father. Within this new framework for her, I came to appreciate many of her finer qualities, qualities that I was able to incorporate into her eulogy. My mother was a loyal, supportive, and loving friend, a wonderful hostess, and a person who took tremendous pride in her cultural heritage—honoring, respecting, and practicing many of its traditions and customs. I also told those assembled at her funeral how she had worked tirelessly so that her children could have a stable home and an opportunity to lead happy and successful lives. Finally, I told how she was a loving and devoted companion to my father. The process of learning about my mother, coupled with my loving and sincere tribute, softened my heart and helped to further heal many of the emotional wounds that she had inflicted upon me as a child. Following her eulogy, I stood in tears before her open casket and gave the customary three bows as a sign of respect. While paying her homage, I silently and gently whispered to her, *"Ma, I've had the last word."* By saying that, I meant to convey to her spirit that my eulogy carried with it the message that it was I who had had the final say regarding our relationship and that I now felt connected to her in warmth, kindness, and gentleness.

Following my mother's death, my father moved in with my oldest brother Martin and his wife, Camilla. I made frequent visits to their home. As a child, I had loved my father only from afar. As we both aged, he shared with me the stories in his life and we grew close in mutual love and admiration until he passed away seven years later. I was honored again when my family asked me to give his eulogy, something that was very easy for me to do. My father epitomized what Confucius called the Superior Man: loving, honorable, charitable, loyal, self-sacrificing, and devoted to the well-being of his family. He also was very fun-loving and had a wonderful sense of adventure and curiosity. Today, I carry him deep within my heart and will often feel that I am honoring and representing him when I am presenting before a group.

Seen and Transformed

The early part of my story revealed that I felt unloved and unwanted, a victim of childhood neglect and verbal abuse. Upon reflection, I now recognize that I also felt somehow defective, that whatever my mother saw in me as repulsive was indeed who I was. As a consequence, I carried in my heart for many, many years the message that *what I presented to people was a façade and that if they saw the real me they would be repulsed*. These negative thoughts were dramatically mitigated at a farewell luncheon for me hosted by my fellow United Way Agency directors when I resigned to take another position. Special among my colleagues were Mary Ann Stalder, Connie Beasley, Al Kovar, and Harry Friedman, all of whom traveled with me during my time at Family Services.

During the luncheon my friends and colleagues lavished me with fond memories of our times together, heartfelt accolades and stories, and creative and genuine expressions of respect for what

I had accomplished for the agency and our community. The outpouring of love elicited from me a deep and passionate outpouring of tears. For the longest time I couldn't stop crying. I felt like a butterfly emerging from his cocoon and spreading his wings for the first time. Engulfed in this joyful moment, I felt I was being validated, appreciated, and seen for who I am for the first time in my life. And although I might not have said it well, I had the same feelings of affection and respect for my colleagues. They were caring, sincere, and compassionate individuals, dedicated to providing the best services possible to our clients. I do remember saying that it was truly an honor to have them in my life and promising that I would always carry their warmth and kindness in my heart with the fondest of memories. I wasn't aware of it at the time, but my experience with them provided another pillar for my forthcoming spiritual transformation. I had changed from a person with serious doubts about my intelligence, skills, talents, and integrity into a person who felt genuine, confident, and psychologically secure.

Peace and Freedom

I would characterize the nearly eight years I spent at the Family Services Association in Riverside as a period of peace and freedom. I grew from an insecure novice into an expert in marital and family therapy. I had reconnected with my parents in an important way. Rosie was very happy working in the field of risk management, making new friends, and reconnecting with her family. Our relationship continued to improve as we worked together to meet the challenges all couples face, negotiating differences and trying to find a balance between work, raising children, our relationship, and meeting other obligations. We liked living in Riverside and considered it our home. We especially enjoyed taking the kids on camping trips to the various national parks, among them Yosemite, Sequoia, Crater Lake, Acadia, Bryce Canyon, and Capitol Reef. Each park possessed its own unique spirit. Each was a reflection of God's infinite beauty. Each was a sanctuary. What I learned later is that my enjoyment of nature is an integral part of my spiritual formation and connection with God.

Evelyn White, one of the preeminent writers in the early years of the Seventh Day Adventist Church, called nature "God's Other Book." She recognized that this book was another pathway through which we could come to know our Lord. Ken Burns, in his breathtaking documentary on the evolution of our national parks, called them "God's Cathedrals." Upon hearing this phrase, I immediately understood my early attraction to these beautiful places. I had been invited by the Holy Spirit into God's very Garden of Eden. The myriad trips our family had taken into national parks across the country were actually spiritual retreats that warmed my heart, graced my soul, and enriched my innermost being in countless ways.

When I immersed myself in nature, the Spirit was again mysteriously working on my behalf; in this instance by nourishing me with creation's infinite beauty. I'll never forget the time, backpacking in Yosemite, when I turned a corner on the trail and found myself in one of the most picturesque landscapes I had ever seen. I was enveloped in what the Indian poet Tagore beautifully expressed in his poem "Transcendence," which I quoted at the beginning of this chapter. In the middle of this paradise was a magnificent waterfall. It was framed by a lovely deep blue sky filled with cumulous clouds, majestic trees, and eye-captivating foliage with flowers of all colors—yellow, red, purple, white, and varying hues of green. Butterflies were flapping their exquisitely-designed and colorful wings, while birds of diverse species danced in the air or sat peacefully on the branches of nearby trees. A gentle breeze spread a wonderful and refreshing fragrance everywhere. All of nature was giving praise and glory to the divine. Caught in feelings of ecstasy, I could not help but join in that celebration. Taking off my backpack and shoes I entered the river in front of the gushing waterfall, raised my arms and tearfully bowed several times, giving honor and praise not only to that which was before me but also to its Creator.

Later on, I came to better understand the meaning of this experience of beauty, recognizing it as a discovery of the sacred and spiritual essence in all creation. I learned that in beauty there is a harmony, wholeness, and sanctity that elicits within us feelings of wonder, warmth, gratitude, and graciousness, as well as the desire to give thanks for the gift of Divine Presence we have just received. Beauty, according to the Irish author John O'Donohue, is inspirational. It momentarily frees us from the habits, routines, and sometime boredom of our daily existence. In the presence of beauty, as in my experience in Yosemite, our hearts are gloriously lit in the light of hope and contemplative joy.

One time when listening to a homily on how God speaks to us, I came to understand why as a child I had mysteriously fallen in love with nature films and, when I had the opportunity to do so, had immersed myself in nature's beauty. The homilist conveyed the message that God conveys his existence to children in an especially warm and gentle manner by exposing them to the beauty and wonder of nature. He speaks to them in a manner they can grasp—experientially rather than intellectually or academically. This was certainly true for me. By giving me the gift of seeing the beauty, richness, and goodness in nature, God was provided me with the lens I needed to see these qualities in all those I was to serve.

> By giving me the gift of seeing the beauty, richness, and goodness in nature, God was provided me with the lens I needed to see these qualities in all those I was to serve.

Moving On

By 1984, we had achieved all the objectives set by the Family Service Association's board of directors when I arrived. The agency's positive reputation in the community had been restored, quality programs and services were being delivered, and it was again financially solvent. I enjoyed the role I played there and decided to remain in the family service movement by moving on to an executive position in a larger agency in Southern California. But once again, my path was redirected by the Holy Spirit.

I had applied for the executive directorship of the Family Services Association of Orange County and was one of the finalists for the position. During the interview with the selection committee, its chairperson indicated that they were interested in having me take the position but had the impression from our conversation that I was more interested in clinical practice, teaching, training, and writing than being an agency executive. An inner voice told me that they were right. I thanked the committee for their consideration and removed my name from the list of candidates.

By the summer of 1985, I had left the Riverside agency and made clinical practice my full time occupation. Shortly thereafter, I opened a family therapy training center with three friends and colleagues, Ben McCloud, Judy Thompson, and Ilene Tilton. We hoped to apply our experience as trainers to enhance the knowledge and skills of other mental health and social service professionals in southern California. After a year's effort, for a variety of reasons, we came to accept the fact that our objectives weren't going to be realized. We ended our partnership and I proceeded with my own clinical practice, teaching, supervising, and providing workshops and training programs.

This period in my life was a time of study and creativity. I began experimenting with many of the major popular models of practice, including those of James Framo, Murray Bowen, Carl Whitaker, Virginia Satir, Carl Rogers, and Albert Ellis. After struggling to blend these varied approaches with the ones I had already mastered, I eventually developed a conceptual framework that allowed me and those I taught to systematically integrate different methods and models of practice into a comprehensive approach. I became an eclectic therapist, able to call upon and adapt several models of practice to address the concerns and issues unique to each individual, family, or couple in counseling. In the process, I began thinking for myself, generating ideas from within regarding human behavior, interpersonal relationships, the therapeutic process, and—most importantly—spirituality. This culminated later in the publishing of my first book, *Constructual Marital Therapy: Theory and Practice*, an accomplishment that I would have never imagined possible in my early years.

My Illusion of Happiness and Fulfillment

I thought at the time that I couldn't have been any happier than I was as I began to fully engage in my private practice and career as an educator and trainer. Every aspect of my life appeared to be in its rightful place. I was blessed with the recognition of my having expertise as a clinician, supervisor, and teacher. These enriching and affirming experiences, coupled with making peace with my parents, silenced and laid to rest my mother's repeated assertion that I was stupid. The Holy Spirit had mysteriously orchestrated my transformation from psychological insecurity to joyful freedom. I was guided to a place where I finally learned to accept myself, to a place where I no longer felt ashamed of my inner landscape. I finally internalized and accepted my gifts and talents, those attributes that Salvador Minuchin and Reverend Hoe had seen so many years before.

But my bubble of success was soon to burst, and the illusion of being happy, fulfilled, and content would be shattered. What had happened is that I had neglected the spiritual dimension of my being. As a consequence, I found myself betraying everyone I loved, cherished or honored—betraying clients, mentors, my profession, my parents, children, Rosie, and God. In so doing I abandoned my integrity, injured and caused pain to those I held most dear, and put myself on a path of spiritual deterioration. I found myself falling into an abyss of emotional, psychological, and spiritual despair.

Chapter 7
Transformation from Religiosity to Spirituality

> Who will separate us from the love of Christ? Will hardship, or distress, or persecution, or famine, or nakedness, or peril, or sword? As it is written,
>
> "For your sake we are being killed all day long, we are accounted as sheep to be slaughtered."
>
> No, in all this we are more than conquerors through him who loved us. For I am convinced that neither death, nor life, nor angels, nor rulers, nor things present, nor things to come, nor powers, nor height, nor depth, nor anything else in all creation, will be able to separate us from the love of God in Christ Jesus, our Lord.
>
> Romans 8:35-39

 During the early period after moving on from the Riverside Family Services Association in 1984, I couldn't have been any happier. It was a period in which I felt successful, professionally competent, and creative. Equally important to me, my father had given me a place of honor in our family, my relationship with Rosie was improving, and I had overcome the sense of shame that had disturbed me throughout my life. One would think I would have been filled with humility and gratitude.

Yet instead of feeling humble, grateful, and indebted for the blessing that had been bestowed upon me and for the emotional and psychological transformation that had taken place, I somehow began to feel the opposite. My success began going to my head, and beneath my conscious awareness my shadow side began emerging, that part of me that is arrogant, envious, and insensitive. I began to move away from being magnanimous towards a path littered with inauthenticity, self-deceit, egocentricity, and moral corruption. I deluded myself into believing that because I was in private practice, serving a middle-class clientele, that I was part of an elite group of clinicians. Instead of using my gifts and talents to serve the well-being of others, I used them to serve conceit and egotism. Instead of listening to my client's stories with my heart, I began listening to them with my head. Instead of seeing my clients as human beings to be served, I saw them as paying customers who needed only my professional help. The façade I had hidden behind came crashing down around me after I betrayed a young woman who, in the midst of desperation, sought my assistance.

Linda, a mother of three young children, was brought in to see me by her mother Ruth, who was concerned about her daughter's depression and suicidal impulses. I quickly learned that Linda's feelings of hopelessness and despair were caused by her rejection and abandonment by Mike, her live-in partner of two years and the father of their six-month-old infant daughter, Ann, Linda's third child.

Mike had abruptly ended the tumultuous relationship, moving in with a woman with whom he was having an affair.

Linda too had a long history of such relationships. Even though she was a respected registered nurse and was obviously attractive, intelligent, warm, and caring, she felt herself to be unattractive, worthless and unlovable.

I was emotionally distant as I listened to her tragic story, one that included tales of the many struggles with her parents and the abusive relationships she had endured. She described the negative feelings she had about herself and the burdens of parenthood that were overwhelming her. In my arrogance, I viewed myself as professionally responsible only for conducting a thorough mental status evaluation to assess the severity of Linda's depression and to access accurately the danger of her suicidal ideations. But my usual feelings of compassion and empathy—previously abundant when dealing with a client like Linda—were strangely absent. She assured me that she would never commit suicide because as she put it, "I would never abandon my children and leave them with the burden of having known that their mother committed suicide." She also signed a "no suicide contract" with me and accepted my recommendation to be evaluated by a psychiatrist for possible pharmaceutical remedies. Finally, she agreed to return in three days to continue her therapy with me. With these assurances, I felt comfortable in sending her home.

Linda missed her appointment three days later. Her mother called to inform me that Linda no longer felt therapy was necessary because Mike had returned and everything was fine. I was pleased on hearing the news. I felt that a burden had been lifted, that now it wasn't necessary for me to spend much time and effort in attending to her needs. My intuition told me that she was still at high risk because of her emotional and psychological vulnerabilities, and I suspected that Mike would leave again, throwing her right back into a state of crisis and depression. But instead of listening to my instincts and making every effort to reach out to Linda and have her return to therapy, I did nothing. My arrogance overshadowed my compassion, wrapped me in a blanket of cold indifference, and had me focus on my needs rather than hers.

My intuition was correct. Six months later Ruth called to inform me that Mike had left again. She asked if she could bring

Linda in the next day. She was once again depressed and suicidal. Linda failed to make the appointment. Late that afternoon Ruth called with the tragic news. Linda committed suicide, after taking the lives of her three children.

    I was shocked and dismayed upon hearing the news and immediately cognizant of the role played by my hubris. I had not only betrayed Linda, but her mother, Linda's children, my profession, those who mentored and instructed me, God, and of course, perhaps worst, myself. At Linda's funeral, I silently made a vow to never again let my arrogance interfere with the way I serve those coming to me for help. To remind me of this vow, I keep the memory of Linda and her children alive in my daily prayers. I am living each day with the regret of my betrayal. As disgraceful as my behavior was, it became still another pillar in my eventual spiritual transformation.

My Shadow Self

I learned from reading the illustrious Swiss psychiatrist Carl Jung his belief that we all have a "shadow," that egotistical, arrogant, and immoral part of us that is selfish, self-serving, and insensitive. Although we are created *in the likeness and image of God* and therefore are fundamentally good, in our imperfect humanity such shadow qualities are intrinsic. According to the teachings of psychology, we tend to find these shadow attributes unacceptable because of the negative and shameful portraits they paint, and we tend to use, normally unconsciously, a variety of coping or psychological defense mechanisms to ignore them. I, for example, have used denial, rationalization, and self-justification to blame Rosie for the many ways I was disrespectful to her. The truth is that I always felt too insecure to admit that part of me was temperamental, insensitive, selfish, and self-righteous.

    I now concur with Jung's theory and believe we will all, at times, entertain our shadow selves. It is intrinsic to our human nature. All of us may, at any given time, find ourselves behaving in a manner that is insensitive, self-serving, and maybe even cruel or immoral. Because our inner self is essentially good, however, these occurrences are generally temporary lapses in our character. My experience with Linda woke me up to the fact that *I was living in my shadow self*, that it had taken over and was leading me down a path of moral decay. My soul was being corrupted, alienating me from my own authenticity and relationship with God.

My failure with Linda taught me the importance of all of us being attentive to, recognizing, and embracing our shadow. Neglecting to do so gives that side of ourselves ever more power and influence. In so doing our inappropriateness will be amplified and perpetuated, keeping us on a path of alienation from ourselves, from others, from God. Acceptance on the other hand, mitigates the negative effects of our shadow, fosters humility, and allows us to embrace our entire humanity. Such acceptance allows us an opportunity for spiritual transformation, that is, the opportunity for the Holy Spirit to enter our hearts and transform us into the loving, compassionate, kind, and gentle people we were created to be. Finally, I learned that acceptance of our shadow selves reminds us of God's unconditional love while implicitly offering us the hope that we can someday live completely in grace and beauty.

Soul Work

The time of peace following the losing and then reclaiming of myself was a blessing. But there was more work to be done. Although I had grown psychologically, intellectually, and emotionally, my issues with God and the Church remained in doubt. I was still imprisoned in the Church's religiosity. I still believed God's love was conditional and that if I made a mistake I might be damned to the eternal fires of Hell. And my relationship with God was still intellectual and resting in fear rather than heartfelt and resting in love.

After beginning to regain the experience of living in the beauty of peace, I found myself facing my greatest challenge. Through my own missteps, I was plunged into the work of the soul. As Sue Monk Kidd wrote, *"And rarely do significant (spiritual) shifts come without a sense of our being lost in dark woods."*[1]

Her words of wisdom certainly applied to me. Like the woman Fatima in the fable, my entire world and reality would once again be turned upside down. I found myself drowning in the dark, tumultuous, and fathomless black hole of spiritual despair. I would have to lose myself before I could be rescued by God's infinite and compassionate love.

I was once again enjoying the fruits of my life when unexpectedly I put my soul and my marriage in peril by betraying Rosie again. In this instance, I opened my heart and allowed myself to become infatuated with a woman I met at a conference. While my unfaithfulness had a predictably devastating effect on Rosie and my children, this misfortune evolved into a spiritually transforming experience, one that would change the way I perceive my marriage, my faith, and my relationship to God.

Although Rosie and I were doing fine, my infatuation with another woman for the first time in our marriage resurrected in me the question of whether or not I married her for love or out of guilt and obligation. It also resurrected what I had thought I'd laid to rest in myself: my belief that if people knew my real character they would think I was a fake. My shadow self would be revealed if I left Rosie to pursue this other relationship. Everyone would see that I wasn't the loving husband and father they perceived me to be; that I wasn't a kind, compassionate, and generous person; that I wasn't a good example of a respected and responsible clinician. Finally, if I separated from Rosie, would God still love me or would I be condemned to Hell?

> My inner voice told me that in order to discover the truth about my marriage and relationship to God, I would have to let go of everything that was dear and meaningful to me.... We have to lose our false self before we can discover our true self.

For months I was tormented by these questions. With my soul begging to be free, I chose to stop hiding and lay to rest the questions that had plagued me since I walked out of the confessional twenty-four years earlier. My inner voice told me that in order to discover the truth about my marriage and relationship to God, I would have to let go of everything that was dear and meaningful to me. In so doing I was, without realizing it, letting go of myself. I had to let go of my professional reputation. I had to let go of what family, friends, and colleagues thought of me. I had to let go of the suffering I would inflict upon my father, children, and Rosie. I would have to let go of my marriage. As painful as it was for me and those I loved, I had to experience what spiritual writers have known throughout the ages—that we have to lose our false self before we can discover our true self.

Listening to my inner voice, I asked Rosie for a separation. This decision would turn out to provide the final pillar for my spiritual transformation. Asking Rosie and then telling Richard, Eileen, and my father of my decision was the most difficult thing I ever did. Rosie was shocked and deeply hurt but, as always, put my needs before hers and supported my request. My children and my father, while disappointed and dismayed, were never critical. And even though friends and family were stunned and saddened upon hearing of our separation, they were tremendously supportive, reaching out to both Rosie and me with love, care, and concern. This display of affection and support was a soothing balm that helped heal what I believed to be a core defect in my character and, in the process, helped me recognize that I didn't have anything to hide. My family and friends conveyed that they knew and loved me for simply being me. I remained tormented nonetheless by the questions of whether or not I loved Rosie and whether or not God would abandon me if I asked her for a divorce.

The Grace of a Spiritual Guide

After I left our family home, I sank deeper into the pain of loneliness, emptiness, and despair, tormented by my inability to discover answers to my questions. In the midst of my anguish, the Holy Spirit sent me a guide. He was Father Sweeney, a Dominican priest and the director of the Saint Andrews Newman Center, an organization devoted to serving the spiritual needs of students attending the University of California at Riverside and Riverside City College. While riding my bike near my new apartment one day, I noticed the Center's storefront sign. I don't know why, but I felt compelled to go through the Center's doors. Listening to my inner voice, I rode over, parked my bike, and entered the building. I was welcomed by Father Sweeney, who happened to be alone and was walking in through the lobby. His friendly greeting instantly put me at ease. Within a short time I was sharing my story with him.

He listened intently with concern, and instead of instructing me to return home to Rosie or giving me permission to divorce her, he suggested that the issues with which I was struggling were between me and God. Only God, the priest said, could give me what I was looking for. He then proceeded to shed light on some of the Church's teachings, most of which were, sad to say, very new to me. Of chief importance was his interpretation of what God was asking of us. I recall him saying that most Catholics are indoctrinated with the principle that we are to "love and obey God." He explained that we are certainly to love God, but before obeying God we have to exercise the gift of our free will. Through a process of discernment, we have to judge for ourselves what we believe to be true regarding the Church's doctrines. In other words, the Church leadership has the responsibility for suggesting how we should live a morally enriching life, but ultimately we must take personal responsibility to discern for ourselves what God is asking of us in a particular situation. This idea reminded me of what the priest at Daylesford Abbey had suggested years earlier, that the Holy Spirit will guide us to what our conscience sincerely determines to be true.

During our time together, Father Michael helped me to understand that such discernment was a process of faith, hope, and love in which we are honestly, openly, and sincerely searching for the truth in that which we're examining. That meant not holding any preconceived answer as to what that truth might be. The process includes the acquisition of knowledge and information, prayer, and reflection, allowing ourselves to be still, quiet, and empty so we can listen as the silent voice of the Holy Spirit guides the entire experience. Before ending our meeting Father

Michael suggested readings that might assist me in my struggles. He also agreed to be my spiritual director.

I was filled with tearful gratitude and appreciation following our meeting. Through the grace of God, I was being provided with the support and guidance that I so desperately needed. And even though I still felt overwhelmed, baffled, and emotionally paralyzed, and even though the answers to my questions remained immersed in a sea of darkness, I now at least possessed the hope that somehow the Holy Spirit would guide me out of my despair.

The following four months I continued to live in anguish and confusion, but with the support of family, friends, Father Michael, and the Holy Spirit, I managed to continue to fulfill my professional responsibilities. I still couldn't face Rosie or the children. I felt I had nothing to say and found it extremely difficult to see and experience the sadness and pain reflected in their faces. Instead, I spent hours alone, reading religious material, praying, and reflecting. I also reread all the love letters Rosie and I had written to each other over the years, and while engaged in this process I tried to reconcile my feelings towards her. One afternoon, while absorbed in this quagmire of confusion, I finally realized that I had betrayed my wife from the onset of our marriage, that I had blamed her for all my insecurities, that I held her responsible for my inability to deal with my fears and insecurities surrounding my relationship with the Church and God. Most significantly, I realized that I was not sincere, as she was, in the sharing of our wedding vows. I wanted to ask her for her forgiveness, but was inhibited by my confusion about my true feelings for her.

In the midst of a sense that I was reaching a breaking point and in dire need of guidance, I arranged to meet with Father Michael, now teaching at St. Mary's College in Moraga just outside San Francisco. The sky was blue and clear and the wind cold and brisk as I drove along the coast on Highway 1 to meet him. Although he was very supportive and understanding, our meeting left me without solace. Leaving his office in spiritual despair and feeling that I might go insane, I found my way to the college chapel, prostrated myself on the floor before the altar and crucifix, and begged God for relief. Two hours later, on my way home, my prayer was answered by a miracle. There is no other word for it.

The Blessings of Freedom

As I was driving home on Highway 1, I was still in emotional despair and praying to God that he pull me out of my spiritual anguish. Before I left the Big Sur area, my prayers were answered with an epiphany. As if struck by lightning, I was suddenly awakened to the realization that God would love and never abandoned me no matter what I did or how I behaved. In that same instant, I realized I loved Rosie with all my heart. I had at last been released from the torment that had plagued me for twenty-four years. I pulled the car over and wept with joy for the gift I had just received.

I didn't recognize until much later that, in that moment of enlightenment, I had finally unraveled the spiritual conundrum encumbering me since that moment in the confessional twenty-four years earlier. Back then I believed I was trapped between honoring my promise to marry Rosie and my promise to obey God. It appeared to be impossible to honor one promise without breaking the other. I recognize now that the issue wasn't about honoring my promises but about love, that what preceded my promises for both was love, that the basis for both my promises was love. I suddenly knew, deep in my heart, that because God is love and because "he who abides in love abides in God and God in him" Rosie and I have always been immersed in God's infinite and transcending love. I never had to choose between my love for Rosie and my love for God. They were one and the same. If I had known all along what I know now, I would have proceeded with our marriage, knowing that I had God's blessing.

After spending some time digesting my newly-received grace and praising and thanking God for his beautiful gift, I turned my attention to Rosie and new questions that now tormented me.

Could she find it in her heart to not only forgive me once again but to reconcile our marriage? Had my decision to separate for a second time been too damaging to our relationship? Could she ever learn to trust me again? Could we ever achieve the level of intimacy we once experienced? My decision to leave the marriage had been based on my own personal and spiritual needs, my search for truth and freedom, but for Rosie, even though she had consented to the separation, it had been another betrayal, another disillusioning experience. I knew that the reality she had constructed over the twenty-three years of our marriage had been disrupted, leaving her angry, confused, disheartened, and in the pit of despair. In this state of mind she must have been asking herself if there was anything real to the relationship we once had. She had never promised she'd be waiting for my return. I had no idea how she was feeling now, whether or not she was already moving on with her life. I got back in the car and starting driving toward her.

The fact that Rosie was an agnostic contributed to my fears. I felt it would be very difficult for her to comprehend my spiritual turmoil; to understand that my struggle was really about my relationship with God and not really about her. From her perspective, the separation was simply about my struggle to be with her or to be with someone else. How could I not love her, she must have thought, given the sacrifices she made so that I could succeed academically and professionally? How could I not love her, she must have thought, given the countless love letters professing my love and the beauty and goodness I said I saw in her? How could I not love her, given the multitude of celebrations, vacations, and adventures we had enjoyed throughout our marriage. How could I not love her, given her unconditional love for me? How could she, lacking a religious foundation upon which to identify with my interior needs and longings, ever fully comprehend my spiritual struggle? Maybe she was right. Maybe I was just kidding myself with all my religious scrupulosity.

With these thoughts, feelings and questions whirling around in my head, I proceeded south to learn if Rosie was willing, as I now was, to continue our marital journey. Adding to my dismay were fears about Richard and Eileen. Had I caused irreconcilable damage to my relationship with my children? My feelings on the way home vacillated wildly between joy and sadness, clarity and confusion, hope and despair, a sense of freedom and a sense of regret, a sense of helplessness and a sense of surrender. It was a time I felt completely powerless and fully at the mercy of the Holy Spirit.

Rosie was pleasantly surprised by my breakthrough, but as I had feared felt too sad, confused, and hurt by our separation to experience the joy that danced within me. She forgave me and agreed to reconcile, but it would take years for her to heal from the pain I had inflicted upon her, pain that I know she still carries in her heart today. It would take years for her to recover the trust in which we once lived. It would take years for her to let down her defenses and allow us to cultivate and fulfill the intimacy we both still desired.

Richard and Eileen, who were tremendously supportive of their mother while I was away, were overjoyed with my return home. Although hurt and confused about my reasons for leaving home, they were forgiving and welcoming. So were my extended family and friends. My fears of alienating them had been groundless.

I was extremely grateful for Rosie's forgiveness and acceptance and have worked diligently to regain her trust. We gradually moved ahead, rebuilding our lives and establishing a new foundation upon which our love could grow. On May 9, 1987, we celebrated our twenty-third wedding anniversary by renewing our vows before our family, friends, and God. Father Michael flew down from Moraga to give God's blessing to the renewal of our vows, which I made joyfully and without reservation this time. As we exchanged our vows, I felt my dream had finally come true, that I was marrying the woman of my heart, the woman I had kissed and held in my arms for the first time on the pier at Pacific Ocean Park twenty-five years earlier, the woman I once again knew I wanted to be with for the rest of my life, the mother of our children.

Illumination and Spiritual Transformation

I later learned that my fear that Rosie's agnosticism would hinder our reconciliation was unwarranted. I made this discovery while delving into the differences and similarities between religion and spiritualty. During this exploration, my eyes were open to the awareness that, while not expressly religious, Rosie is, in fact, a deeply spiritual person. I also recognized the fact that while religion implies boundaries, spirituality transcends any and all limitations. Within the metaphysical realm anything is possible. In fact, participating in a religious tradition may not have anything to do with spirituality. We need only look at the display of hate and atrocities committed in the name of God and religion since the beginning of civilization, or to glance at our morning newspapers today, to understand this.

In my study of religion and spirituality I also came to believe that spirituality, which I define as possessing the loving spirit of God, must precede organized religion. Referring again to the opening of John's Gospel gives credence to my belief that *"In the beginning was the Word, and the Word was with God, and the Word was God."* I have come to discover that spirituality at the deepest level doesn't rest in religious beliefs, doctrines, or practices, but rather in a loving, gentle, compassionate, forgiving, magnanimous, devotional, and self-sacrificing heart. With this discovery I came to recognize that I was describing Rosie's essence, that this was Rosie. While I struggled so publicly with issues of religion, Rosie was the one who has always remained spiritually centered.

Rosie and I, like all couples, have differences that cause disturbances and create disappoints in our relationship. But her spirituality and its inherent supernatural qualities allowed us to eventually fulfill our desire for an enriching and intimate relationship. Her gentleness, coupled with her love, would never permit her to knowingly hurt, reject, or treat me with indifference. Even though she couldn't comprehend my religious struggle, her compassion allowed her to join in my despair and anguish. Her magnanimity transcended her own pain, suffering, and disillusionment, allowing her to forgive me for my betrayal and the grief I inflicted upon her. And her devotion not only to me but to her parents and our children has always allowed her to put her family's hopes, dreams, and desires before her own. In addition to faith, hope, and love, she truly is God's most precious gift to me.

Father Michael suggested that before returning to St. Mary's later in the year I attend a 30-Day Ignatian silent directed retreat at the Jesuit Retreat Center in Los Altos, California. The focus of such retreats is to live intentionally for a month in the Divine Presence. It is a time that allows the Holy Spirit, through our prayer, reflection, self-examination, and discernment, to guide us toward a greater understanding of ourselves and lead us to a deeper, richer, and more endearing relationship with God. To engage in this process, explained Father Michael, required entering the retreat with no definite expectations and instead to humbly surrender and be open to whatever path the Holy Spirit chose. I remember remarking to him that what he suggested sounded nice but I didn't have a clue as to what he really meant. Nevertheless, as best as I could, I entered the retreat with no expectations, acquiescing to the experience that was to follow.

From the moment I stepped onto the retreat grounds, I felt bathed in love. I was enthralled by the beauty of the center itself, lovely and peaceful, a prayerful natural environment in which to contemplate in the presence of God. On the grounds were magnificent trees and many varieties of colorful flowers, trails on which to stroll, and hidden alcoves in which to be alone. I felt the acceptance of the spiritual directors who were caring, compassionate and inviting, providing a safe environment in which we could later share our thoughts and feelings. The lectures and homilies they gave were excellent and informative, providing an inspiring context in which to enter the thirty days of silence.

In socializing and becoming acquainted with my fellow retreatants, I basked in their warmth, kindness, and friendship. Even though we didn't have any verbal communication for nearly thirty days, we were all being embraced in God's embrace and, as a consequence, we communicated and connected with one another at the soul level. When we came out of silence a month later, we all mysteriously experienced a deep sense of connection and intimacy.

Upon entering the silence, I continued to be comforted by the beauty of the Divine Presence. Each day was blessed with spiritual experiences, experiences I could never adequately capture in words. There were days of consolation and days of desolation, days in which I experienced untold joy and days I experienced deep sadness, days I was engulfed in divine intimacy and days I was sinking into despair, days I was blessed with mystical experiences and days I experienced extreme loneliness, days I rested in solitude and days I struggled in turmoil, days I felt alive and days in which I encountered death. It would take another whole book for me to explain these experiences, so it must suffice to say here that the Holy Spirit took me on a journey into the deepest recesses of my soul, revealing and allowing me to experience truths I never knew about my life, my relationships, especially with Rosie, and—most importantly—my connection with God. In the process I entered into a deep, intimate, and personal relationship with God. For the first time in my life I experienced living and resting in the loving embrace of Our Lord.

> For the first time in my life I experienced living and resting in the loving embrace of Our Lord.

Going to confession during the retreat was a profound corrective experience. For the first time I felt surrounded by safety, forgiveness and compassion. For the first time there was no "confessional" in which there was a barrier placed between me and the person to whom I was confessing. I was face to face with God's representative, experiencing the fullness of the Divine Presence in the form of another human being. I experienced this confession as an invitation and blessing rather than a condemnation, judgment, or something to dread. Because of the retreat's emphasis on truthful soul searching, I was absolutely clear that I was being sincere in the acknowledgment of my transgressions. I wept in sadness for having betrayed God's love and trust with my selfish and self-serving acts, acts which not only tarnished my soul but caused injury to others. For the first time ever, I felt spiritually cleansed and unburdened while experiencing the healing power of God's infinite love.

My experiences during the retreat were transforming, providing me with the opportunity to experience the true meaning of faith, hope, and love, something that had escaped me all my life. My faith was transformed from that of one immersed in the darkness of ignorance to that of one dancing in the illumination of understanding, from a faith that emphasized an attachment to a list of rules and regulations to a faith that emphasized the freedom to exercise my free will and discern for myself how to respond to God's call to live a spiritual life, and from a faith that emphasized a judgmental God living somewhere outside of me to a loving God who dwells within my hearts. My hope in God was transformed from a hope that was shallow and self-serving, trying to earn my way into heaven, to a hope that is deep, one that emphasizes God's invitation to live a spiritually-meaningful and enriching life while here on earth. And my love for God was transformed from servile to filial, from a love founded on intimidation and fear to one founded on freedom, gratitude, and humility.

At the retreat, I also became aware of the fact that hope is shrouded in mystery, that there is no way I can predict the future events that will eventually shape, organize, and transform me. With this awareness I recognized that God, through the intercession of the Holy Spirit, had been present with me all along, providing me with loving relationships, mentors, and education to help me overcome the emotional wounds and psychological insecurities associated with my upbringing. I recognized that nothing in my life has been accidental, that the suffering I experienced and overcame has been part of my spiritual formation, and that I have been directed towards my life's work, my vocation, by my career choices and the opening of the many unexpected doors of opportunity through which I have passed. It has become very evident to me that my purpose in life was to live in authenticity and in so doing to serve those in need of mental health, social service, and child welfare programs. All my acquisition of knowledge, skills, training, and credentials throughout the years was meant to be used toward this end.

Conversion of Manner

The experience at the retreat planted the seeds for what Thomas Merton called "a conversion of manner," a conversion in which I would begin behaving in a manner that put the will of God and the needs of my fellow human beings, no matter what the relationship, before my own. In so doing, I recognized that I would be accepting the invitation to make God the center of my heart and my life rather than what I had been doing previously, which was to keep him at a distance. With this recognition I began cultivating my conversion by reading spiritual literature, broadening my devotional practices, and going on regular retreats.

One of the most influential books in my efforts at growing spiritually was *Out of Solitude* by Henri Nouwen. In it he describes how Christ routinely withdrew and sought solitude to be with his Father before returning to his busy ministry. I took Jesus' example to heart and began routinely taking extended retreats that included attending a 30-Day Ignatian Retreat every five years and even sitting alone in the desert once for forty days. While in solitude, I took the time to reflect on, digest, and integrate what I was learning from my various experiences. I would simply rest and be with God before returning to my responsibilities and duties.

As part of my conversion process, I also took it upon myself to become a more informed Catholic by immersing myself in the study of the Catholic Church. As a result I have gained a greater understanding and profound appreciation of her history, evolution, and practices. I also studied other major faith traditions, especially Zen Buddhism. My explorations have helped me to recognize that by living a spiritual life, I would become, as many Native Americans and Aborigines are, more aware of and present to the Divine Presence in all creation. My studies and reflections have also helped me to recognize and embrace the fact that God is inclusive rather than exclusive and that my faith tradition is only one of many paths that can guide us toward living a spiritually enriching, loving, and hopeful life.

Living in Hopefulness

As the years have passed since my first 30-Day Ignatian Retreat, I have learned to live in the present and in hopefulness, not trying to control my destiny but instead surrendering to and having faith in what God has planned for me. In so doing, I have become comfortable with allowing life to unfold and reveal its secrets to me. Doors have continued to open and close, but rather than seeing the closing of doors as obstacles, I now see them as opportunities for personal and spiritual growth, as opportunities for redirecting my life in a manner that will be more fulfilling and enriching.

I have always found Romans 8:35-39, the Bible passage at the beginning of this chapter, to be inspirational. It offers a pronouncement on hope, the message in this book, and God's unconditional love for us. Upon reflecting on my spiritual journey, I can relate to it even more, embracing its message at a deeper and more meaningful level. My experience has taught me that neither being unloved and rejected by my mother nor the religiosity of the Catholic Church, neither being abandoned in confession nor my own scrupulosity, neither my betrayals nor my ignorance, neither my sinfulness nor pathological fear of God, neither my selfishness nor my temptations, neither the seductions of the world nor any other influences trying to tear me from the love of my God have prevented him from reaching out and touching, nourishing, and enriching my soul. Nothing has prevented God from enveloping me in infinite and encompassing love. I certainly haven't done anything to earn or deserve this. It has all been pure gift.

Chapter 8
Evolution into a Spiritually Based Practitioner

To say I love you with authenticity
says it's wonderful that you exist in the world.

UNKNOWN WRITER

 I have shared how it became evident during my first Ignatian Retreat that my purpose in life was to serve those in need of mental health, child welfare, and social services. Upon further reflection, I discovered that my personality and experiences in life have prepared me for my evolution into a spiritually based practitioner and spiritual director. My deep feelings of loneliness, shame, and alienation, as painful and disheartening as they were, have cultivated within my heart compassion and empathy for the pain and suffering of others. My endless hours sitting alone as a child in the corner of my living room watching the activities of my family have honed my observational skills and ability to sit quietly, comfortably, and patiently while allowing human drama to unfold before me. Listening to the stories of my siblings while sitting by my mother at the dinner table, afraid to speak, has prepared me to be a good listener and to remain attentive to the stories of those I serve. It also taught me to be comfortable with taking in information from multiple conversations occurring simultaneously, an attribute necessary for being an effective family and group therapist. The "threat stress" associated with my feelings of shame has been transformed into "challenge stress," which cultivated within me creativity, mental sharpness, and my attention to detail, characteristics which contributed to my being an effective leader, teacher, and presenter. Furthermore, my being a dreamer has prepared me to encourage others to dream and thereby offered them renewed hope. And my natural attraction to the Church's rituals and symbols has planted in me the seeds for developing and using rituals and symbols in my practice. In addition, the fact that I am an introvert has contributed to my ability to be imaginative, reflective, and thoughtful; attributes that are part of the foundation upon which I have built my work. Finally, being raised in a traditional Chinese family and living among varied ethnic and racial groups has made it easy for me to naturally identify with and work among widely diverse populations.

    I also have discerned that nothing in my career path was accidental, that I was led unknowingly into discovering my vocation and, in the process, discovering myself. Throughout my professional livelihood there were many unexpected career changes, so many times when I thought I was heading in one direction that a door opened unexpectedly in another.

Finally, I have described how I was guided out of my cold, dark, confusing shadow of despair about my marriage into the heartwarming radiant light of life and comforting embrace of God's enduring love and kindness, and how my participation in the Ignatian Retreat evolved into a spiritually transforming experience. I began to see and experience my clinical work differently and began to look at my work through a spiritual lens. Flowing out of this shift emerged the idea of developing a spiritually based practice. This shift happened to coincide with a major shift taking place in clinical practice, the integration of religion and spirituality into our work. Numerous articles and books have begun to emerge in our professional literature addressing this subject.

In an effort to design a paradigm for a spiritually based practice I began to review this literature and attend workshops that addressed this topic. I found myself studying the similarities and differences between the major spiritual traditions to assist me in my search. I paid particular attention to examining the similarities, differences, and interrelatedness among psychological, religious, and spiritual disciplines.

Most important to me, however, was that I relied upon my Ignatian Retreat experience in providing ideas for what I was searching for. I recall finding myself becoming a participant observer during the retreat, observing the principles and interventions of my spiritual director. I couldn't help notice the similarities between clinical practice and spiritual direction. Although the former addressed temporal issues associated with finding peace and happiness in our daily lives, and the latter addressed spiritual issues associated with cultivating a deeper and more enriching relationship with God and our fellow human beings, many of the interventions and principles of practice were similar. I gained an awareness of how the process in which I was involved not only had a major influence on me spiritually, but psychologically as well. Upon reflection, I came to recognize that St. Ignatius was a natural psychologist and that of course God, who was directing Ignatius, is the ultimate psychotherapist. With this recognition I came to the conclusion that what is spiritually sound and relevant must be also be psychologically and interpersonally meaningful. That is, living a spiritually enriching life coincides with living a psychologically meaningful one as well. Otherwise spiritual concepts and practices wouldn't have any temporal significance or value.

For me living a spiritually enriching life, one that enhances, illumines, and informs all dimensions of ourselves, would be living in what the Church calls the "Fruits of the Spirit." Those fruits are love, joy, peace, patience, kindness, gentleness, good counsel, and generosity. It stands to reasons that living in these spiritual attributes and domains can only enhance and illumine our psychological and emotional well-being. Living in love allows us to form and cultivate intimate, affirming, and enriching relationships. Living in joy allows us to celebrate and be enriched by the beauty that is always before us. Living in peace allows our mind, body, emotions, and spirit to rest in harmony. Living in patience allows us to be present in the here and now while looking hopefully towards the future. Living in kindness allows us to breathe in warmth, emotional freedom, and mercy. Living in good counsel allows and encourages us to grow psychologically, emotionally, creatively, and spiritually. Living in generosity allows for and perpetuates compassion, altruism, and caring for the well-being of others. In short, living in the Fruits of the Spirit allows us to feel safe and secure, be enriched by all the goodness this world has to offer, and live in gratitude for the abundance that has been bestowed upon us.

> Living in the Fruits of the Spirit allows us to feel safe and secure, be enriched by all the goodness this world has to offer, and live in gratitude for the abundance that has been bestowed upon us.

It also stands to reason that if our clients in therapy were in touch with and embraced their spiritual dimensions, their decisions, choices, and behaviors would adjust accordingly. Consequently, it also stands to reason that they would address the problems and issues they brought to therapy by making wiser and more prudent decisions, decisions based in truth, decisions that honor their integrity, decisions that nurture their souls.

Faith, Love...and Hope

In a recent workshop I conveyed to the participants that the most important attribute we bring to our practice is our intelligence, knowledge, talents, skills, and beliefs. My beliefs of course have been centered in my Catholicism, which springs from the supernatural virtues of faith, love...and hope. I increasingly have grown in a living faith that recognizes that the Divine Presence dwells within me (and all of us), allowing us to see and experience the beauty that is always there. I also have lived in a hope that assures me that no matter how confounding my circumstances I can always find peace and solitude. I have lived in the love of my Creator, friends, family, and colleagues. For me, the heart and foundation of a spiritually based practice is predicated upon these three supernatural virtues that inform and guide my life.

I came to realize that a spiritually based practitioner does not have to be a Catholic or, for that matter, a believer in any particular religious tradition. Rather, a spiritually based practitioner must believe in the essence or spirit inherent in the virtues of faith, love, and hope. They must have faith in and see the loving qualities or interior goodness that lies within everyone they are called to serve. Sometimes this isn't so easy to do, given some of the horrendous things our clients do: sexual assault, abusing and neglecting children, even committing murder. Nevertheless, no matter what issues our clients bring to therapy, or what they may have done, we must be able to separate the person from their problems and behaviors, see their loving qualities, and treat them with care and loving kindness.

At a deeper level I believe a spiritually based practitioner must have a faith in a Divine Presence that is looking after our well-being by stitching into the fabric of our essence an interior goodness. Among the many ways that goodness is expressed is in loving kindness, self-sacrifice, and magnanimity. I also believe that we should feel that this Divine Presence continuously invites us to live in our interior goodness and has provided us with the hope and capacity to overcome life's challenges so that we may do so. Finally, I believe spiritually based practitioners must have faith that we are gifted with the ability to assist our clients in recognizing, claiming, and embracing their authenticity and the beautiful person they were created to be.

I began this chapter with the following truism, *"To say I love you with authenticity is to say it's wonderful that you exist in this world."* In other words, love is the ultimate affirmation and is associated with our very existence. To feel and live in love allows us to see and experience all the goodness this world has to offer. Yet, like me, so many of our clients' problems, insecurities, and feelings of worthlessness can be attributed to their being treated with indifference, feeling unloved, or worse, feeling that they are unlovable. Therefore I believe that spiritually based practitioner must recognize that we are in the business of love, treat all our clients with loving kindness, and help those feeling unloved or unworthy of love to correct their mistaken perception.

And finally, I have come to see that a spiritually based practitioner must also recognize that we are in the business of hope and must be hopeful, even when there appears to be no hope. To provide understanding for this paradox I learned from my readings to distinguish between temporal and spiritual or mystical hope, the former emanating from our "rational self" while the latter from our soul or "spiritual self." The former is "hoping for" something, while the latter is "hoping in" a force that governs the universe. The former is acquired. Its origins are loosely rooted in our physical world. The latter is infused, with origins rooted deep in our metaphysical universe. The former functions in the realm of the concrete, where there appear to be answers to what is being hoped for; the latter resides in the realm of elusiveness and mystery, in which there appear to be no solutions. The former can be realized through assistance and rational planning, while the latter is revealed through epiphanies and grace. Spiritual hope begins where temporal hope ends. This idea may be hard to grasp, but according to Brother David Steindl-Rast such hope is real because it is supernatural virtue and its steadfastness and reality is "anchored in the heart."

Spiritually Based Practice

In addition to recognizing the importance of faith, love, and hope in my formulation of a spiritually based practice, I also recognized that such an approach had to go beyond what I have been formally trained to do, which is to diagnose and treat my clients presenting problems. This, of course, didn't mean that I had to discard what I had learned regarding personal and interpersonal growth and development. Nor did it mean dispensing with the major principles regarding clinical practice, principles such as being supportive, client-centered, transparent, emphasizing strengths rather than deficits, fostering a safe and collaborative atmosphere, respecting our clients' right of self-determination, and assisting them in addressing the issues they bring to therapy. Instead, a spiritually based therapy means attending to both my clients' temporal needs and spiritual well-being simultaneously and understanding the relationship between the two. It also means utilizing spiritual principles of practice and interventions along with conventional ones. Finally, it means guiding clients to recognize and embrace their interior goodness, that is, those virtuous dimensions of themselves that are loving, compassionate, kind, caring, generous, forgiving, and hopeful.

For guidance in these areas I turned to what I had learned from attending my first Ignatian Retreat. I recognized of course that the purpose and goal of clinical practice and spiritual direction are very different. Nevertheless I felt that in addition to faith, hope, and love, I could glean other ideas and principles that would be useful in my search. Proceeding with this in mind, I was able to take and apply the following five ideas around which to organize my conceptual framework. I have concluded that together they provide the pathway to speaking to and addressing the spirituality of those I serve.

The first principle of spiritually based practice is having a compassionate presence, a presence that was shown to me throughout my retreat. The second principle is placing an emphasis on listening and responding rather than diagnosing and treating those I serve. The third principle is, like my spiritual directors, being prudent by listening to what is in the hearts of those seeking my assistance. The fourth principle is integrating into the therapeutic process meditation, reflection, and religious and spiritual rituals and symbols. Finally, I have found that the Ignatian Exercises are not only involved in the process of discovery but also in the process I call spiritual healing. In addition to helping our clients find solutions to their presenting problems, spiritually based practitioners should also be involved in the practice of healing spiritual wounds.

A Compassionate Presence

One of the things that impressed me most at my retreat was the compassionate presence demonstrated by my spiritual director, Father Fellon, who I knew was the vehicle through which the Holy Spirit was guiding me. The retreat is an immersion in The Spiritual Exercises of St. Ignatius of Loyola, in which much of the retreat time is focused on either an examination of conscience or meditation on our sins. During these exercises, we explored and examined closely our immoral tendencies and behaviors, those things that alienate us from our interior goodness, our fellow human beings, and God. As part of the process we wrote in our journals what we had discovered and then shared those discoveries with our spiritual director. Needless to say, sharing these confidential, secret, and private details of our lives can elicit deep feelings of embarrassment, shame, and guilt. However, with Father Fellon, I never felt judged or was made to feel uncomfortable. Instead, I only experienced loving kindness, concern for my well-being, and support for the struggles and challenges I was facing. His gentleness, warmth, understanding, and compassion provided an environment in which I felt safe to explore those areas of my life that had impeded my spiritual growth and to develop a more intimate relationship with my Creator and those I love and serve.

In addition to Father Fellon's loving kindness, I also experienced the Divine Presence throughout the retreat—in my moments of prayer, walks in the garden, participation in the Liturgy, mystical experiences, and most compellingly during my act of confession. These experiences allowed me to feel loved, accepted, affirmed, and healed. Compassion, therefore, had to become one of the touchstones for my conceptualization of a spiritually based practice. I want those I serve to experience what I had experienced in the beauty of a compassionate relationship.

Through my experience at the retreat, I recognized that compassion was more about a way of "being with" than "doing for" those we serve, although what often flows from this heartfelt expression of love is some form of action.

> I recognized that compassion was more about a way of "being with" than "doing for" those we serve, although what often flows from this heartfelt expression of love is some form of action.

My work with a young woman named June illustrates such a presence. First I had to help her overcome her insecurity and the negative feelings she had about herself. These feelings were, in part, due to the rejection and negative messages she received from her parents, particularly her mother, in her formative years. They could also be attributed to poor decisions June made in her young adult life, decisions that caused her extreme emotional pain and suffering.

Then I had to assist June in removing the emotional barrier between her and her mother. It was a painful process, with June finding herself grieving over the loss of what should have been a happy and enriching childhood. However, through this disturbing and sad process she was able to find acceptance of what had happened in her upbringing and was able to emerge feeling healed and at peace. Adding to her peace was the comfort she found in forgiving her mother for all of her wrongdoing, an act that also put them on the path of reconciliation.

But just when all seemed well, June received the devastating news that she had cancer. In this chapter of her life she found herself facing her greatest challenge, encountering the possibility she might be facing immanent death. Soon after receiving the tragic news, my heart sank when I saw June standing sadly alone in the middle of her hospital room, waiting to hear about the extent of her cancer and to make a decision about whether treatment would be necessary. I knew nothing I could say would provide her with comfort. Instead of either of us speaking, we gently embraced and were joined in compassion. In other words, we became *companions in pain*. The relationship was reciprocal, with me offering her care, warmth, and loving kindness in her moment of sadness and despair and me in return receiving from her the gifts of her vulnerability and trust. She immediately began crying, allowing the heaviness of her emotions to be released and shared. For a long while, I softly rubbed the back of her shoulders while her tears continued to flow. I was hoping that she would feel just a little more safe, comforted, and nurtured. Finding some measure of relief, June was able to release me from our embrace and we were able to explore her feelings regarding the ordeal ahead.

I have come to believe that stitched into the fabric of compassion are feelings of hopefulness, for at the core of compassion is Divine love, and love and hope are inseparable. Experiencing a compassionate presence carries with it the hope that we won't be abandoned in our pain and suffering; that there will be caring and loving individuals who will provide us with support, guidance, assistance, and nurturing in our time of need and distress; that there are those in the world who will, if necessary, supply us with the resources to help rebuild or reconstruct our lives. Compassion, no matter under what circumstances or how it is expressed, joins us in a loving manner at the deepest level, offering us hope that everything will somehow be better in the future. I believe this is why compassionate presence is at the heart of all major religious traditions and an experience to which everyone can identify and relate.

Listening and Responding

In our clinical training, we are taught to be assertive and actively engage our clients by asking questions that will, based on our model of treatment, help diagnose and assess their problems and needs. Based on our assessment, we work collaboratively in developing a treatment plan. Having formulated our plan, we use our experience and expertise in making interventions that will achieve established therapeutic goals.

The process in spiritually based practice is different. What I noticed in my relationships with Father Michael and Father Fellon was not only their compassionate presence but their *passive stance*. Rather than taking the initiative and asking a series of probing questions based on some diagnostic template, they gently encouraged me to share not only thoughts and feelings but also my story and what was in my heart. Ernest Kurtz and Katherine Ketcham, in their book, *The Spirituality of Imperfection*, have this important insight: "I learned that listening to and acknowledging a person's story was the surest way of touching their spirit." Both of my early spiritual directors, Father Michael and Father Fellon, would sit quietly and listen and only after having listened attentively and respectively would they respond in a manner that was spontaneous, understanding, and affirming. This process allowed me to feel safe, comfortable, and acknowledged. It also allowed me to feel that I was being treated as a unique human being with virtues as well as imperfections. Finally, their form of engagement fostered the use of my own intuitive wisdom in addressing what I had shared.

I felt what I learned from those two men could be incorporated in my approach to spiritually based practice. My first task is to honor the uniqueness of my clients' human and spiritual nature and the circumstances in which they find themselves. I have to listen not only to my clients' presenting concerns but also to what is in their hearts. I must take a quiet and non-intrusive position while listening attentively to their story and then—like a concert violinist who naturally, creatively, and intuitively expresses the musical scores practiced and internalized over the years—respond naturally, creatively, and spontaneously, calling upon and using the body of knowledge, skills, and intuition I have acquired throughout my career. Every client is to be treated not only with honor and respect but also within the context of his or her unique spiritual nature. The issues and concerns clients bring to therapy are to be treated in the same manner, in their own context. The underpinnings of a spiritually based practice are founded in a process that is heartfelt and not strategic, spontaneous and not manipulative, organic and not prescriptive, creative and not contrived. The following narrative should shed light on this.

> The underpinnings of a spiritually based practice are founded in a process that is heartfelt and not strategic, spontaneous and not manipulative, organic and not prescriptive, creative and not contrived.

Sixteen-year-old Crystal was brought to see me by her mother because she had been sexually assaulted. It was evident in our meeting that Crystal was sad, depressed, and fearful. Other than mentioning that she no longer had any friends and that she had become a couch potato, Crystal remained silent while her mother shared her concerns and the details of the tragic incident. Those included fears that Crystal might remain depressed and miss the opportunity to enjoy her adolescence and that she would continue to feel so physically and emotionally damaged that she would be unable to develop a normal relationship with men. Knowing that the pathway for gaining Crystal's trust and confidence was providing an atmosphere in which she felt safe, nurtured, and supported, I requested that her initial visits take place without her mother present.

During the first session, Crystal remained silent. Again, it was evident that she was withdrawn. I simply responded to her silence by saying, "You look so sad, Crystal. Is there anything you would like to talk about?" Looking down at her hands she remained silent. Having learned from the Ignatian Retreat the power and influence of sitting in loving silence, I intuitively decided not, as I normally would have done, to actively attempt to draw her out. Instead, I joined in her sadness. That is, I entered her silence with compassion and remained silent. After approximately ten to twelve minutes, I again shared with her my feelings that she looked very sad and asked if she would like to share anything with me. She continued to remain silent. Respecting her decision, I again joined in her sadness by also continuing to remain silent. After some time had passed, I once again mentioned her sadness and asked if she had any questions of me. She remained silent, as did I. Finally, I broke our silence by sharing with her that I needed to end our time together. And then before shaking her hand, I thanked her for allowing me to sit with her in her sadness.

The weekend following our session I happened to be relaxing in Solvang, a small Dutch tourist community on the coast of California, when I walked into a store in which they were selling couch potato dolls. Upon seeing them, I thought of Crystal and how she might like having such a companion. I bought it, wrapped it as a gift, and along with a gift card and a poem I wrote regarding friendship, gave it to her at the beginning of our next session. The gift and card, which said she would never have to be alone again, was a surprise that brought tears to her eyes. After reading my poem and opening her gift, she stood up, reached out, and thanked me while giving me a warm hug. For whatever reasons, my thoughtfulness and loving gesture allowed Crystal's sadness, for just a moment, to be transformed into joy. A few minutes later, while holding on tightly to her new doll, she began sharing her painful story.

There is a Buddhist saying that "Words fragment. In silence there is union." In retrospect, I feel that in our silence, Crystal and I were immersed in a loving union, one in which we were being experientially, emotionally, and spiritually joined in the beauty of her tender sadness. I also believe that by remaining silent and respecting her privacy, I gained some measure of respect and trust. Finally, by thanking her for allowing me to sit with her in solitude, I was sending the message that I was present to her and her suffering. The gift of the doll not only reinforced this message, but also symbolically illustrated that I carried her in my heart. My poem on friendship convinced her that she had a friend with whom she could walk in her pain. The gift and the poem together conveyed the message that I could be trusted and would address her fears and vulnerabilities with sensitivity, respect, gentleness and compassion. They also carried the message of hope that I could somehow assist her in finding a way out of her pain and turmoil. By accepting my gift she would, with me as her guide, walk on the path of hopefulness, a path that would eventually lead to her physical and psychological well-being.

Prudence

The major objective of traditional therapy has always been to assist our clients in meeting their temporal needs by helping them resolve the problems they bring to us. While certainly adhering to this objective, spiritually based practice, as I have conceived it, also works at a deeper spiritual level. In reaching for this deeper level, we pay homage to our clients' authenticity, the self that God created us to be, the self that lives in such virtues as integrity, courage, generosity, and patience. The path through which this is accomplished is prudence, which is speaking in a manner that touches and penetrates people's hearts by recognizing, acknowledging, and validating their interior goodness. During this discourse we hope they will be able to recognize and embrace the inner goodness that has always existed in them, but for a variety of reasons has gone unrecognized or unappreciated.

I recall working with sixteen-year-old Manuel, who was living in a group home and on probation for dealing in drugs, vandalism, and burglary. Before being removed from his home, he lived with his drug-addicted mother Sonya, a younger sister, Maya, of whom he was very protective, and Gregory, his mother's live-in boyfriend of nine months. According to Manuel, his mother frequently brought home men who were often verbally and sometimes physically abusive. In trying to protect his mother, he told Gregory that if he ever abused his mother he could "kick the shit out of him." Also living with them, before she died, was his grandmother, with whom he had a close relationship. In her memory, he wore a cross she gave him.

During a home visit, Manuel attacked Gregory after seeing him push his mother. In the ensuing brawl, he accidentally kicked Maya, causing her to suffer a concussion and lose two front teeth. A short time later he knocked his antagonist's head against the end of the dinner table, leaving him unconscious. Not wanting to jeopardize his probationary status, Sonya told him to go into his bedroom and let her take responsibility for what had happened. Reluctantly he acquiesced to her demands. After she called 911 Gregory awoke with only a slight concussion.

In reporting the incident, Manuel was extremely angry, berating both himself and his mother. He felt that he was, as he put it, "a pussy" (his word for being a coward) for letting his mother take the blame for what had happened. He also said he "felt like shit" (his phase for feeling guilty) for causing his sister injury. He also exclaimed, "Why does my mother have to be such a whore?" (his words for her promiscuity.) Instead of focusing on the incident and what other therapists might have deemed inappropriate behavior (losing his temper and fighting) and disrespectful language (calling his mother a whore), I chose to look into and speak to his heart and to point out his admirable qualities. Among the things I tried to convey was that he was loving and loyal—as demonstrated by the relationships with his grandmother and sister and his efforts at protecting his sister and mother. In addition, I shared with him that the wearing of his grandmother's cross was an indication that he was spiritual and that by defending his mother he was courageous. I went on to say that he was highly moral, which was evident by his feeling bad for hurting his sister and seeing that his mother's sexual behavior was inappropriate. In short, I worked at conveying to Manuel that I recognized and respected his admirable qualities, qualities that I suspect had only been acknowledged by his grandmother.

One of the major things I learned from my personal life, clinical training, and experience at my Ignatian Retreats is that our internal—often unconscious—beliefs about ourselves have a major influence in our decision making, feelings, and behaviors. It naturally follows that if my clients are able to recognize and embrace their authenticity they will live accordingly, making prudent decisions and behaving in a manner that contributes to their own well-being, that of others, and of the world at large. If I could have Manuel embrace his beautiful qualities, it would follow that he would trust and allow me to guide him on a path that would lead to a successful, enriching and hopeful life.

Spiritual Rituals and Symbols

All major religious traditions stitch into their spiritual practices the use of meditation, reflection, rituals, and symbols. These features serve many purposes, among them putting us in touch with our interiority; providing us with the means to add a rich texture to our lives; creating a sanctuary in which we can feel safe and secure; trying to make concrete things that are really invisible and incomprehensible; and connecting us at a deeper level with both those we love and with the Divine Presence. For me, for example, my daily devotional practice of meditating and reflecting on the Stations of the Cross serves these purposes.

For those unfamiliar with this Catholic tradition, the Stations of the Cross represent Christ's passion, crucifixion, and death. The fourteen stations that depict his journey can be found on the walls of most Catholic churches. When I am unable to attend a church to follow the Stations, I travel the journey in quiet reflection and prayer.

The first station begins with Jesus being condemned by Pilate, the second with him carrying the cross, the third with him falling the first time, the fourth with him meeting his mother, the fifth with him being helped by Simon, the sixth with him being shown compassion by Veronica, the seventh with him falling a second time, the eighth with him comforting the women of Jerusalem, the ninth with him falling the third time, the tenth with him being stripped, the eleventh with him being nailed to the cross, the twelfth with him suffering and dying on the cross, the thirteenth with him being taken down from the cross, and the fourteenth with him being laid to rest in the tomb. With the exception of his condemnation, crucifixion, death and burial, the rest of the stations depict moments that are historically questionable and strictly matters of faith.

For me, whether or not the stations are an accurate interpretation of the events of the time is not important. What is important is that, through the corridor of faith, each station brings to life and makes tangible that which is really intangible and incomprehensible. They bring to my life God's infinite love and devotion to me and my spiritual and temporal well-being. What is important to me is that the stations elicit within me deep feelings of being comforted, loved, and affirmed. As I stand or kneel before each station I cannot help but reflect upon my behavior and God's Divine Presence. Finally, informed by faith and hope, I know I am being influenced by the Holy Spirit in ways I cannot imagine and that each time I answer Christ's call to journey with him my faith is cultivated and blossoms. My love for God and my fellow human beings is enriched and deepened.

> The Stations of the Cross bring to my life God's infinite love and devotion to me and my spiritual and temporal well-being.... Each time I answer Christ's call to journey with him my faith is cultivated and blossoms.

It would naturally follow that knowing the importance of religious and spiritual rituals, symbols, and metaphors in my own life that I would then appropriately weave them into my spiritually based practice. Such an instance arose when I began seeing Gloria, a thirty-nine year old Hispanic teacher who, after two years, was still grieving over the tragic loss of her only child, Leticia, who died in a car accident at the age of fifteen. Gloria was continuing to feel overwhelmed with feelings of depression, loneliness, emptiness, and hopelessness. She also found herself crying uncontrollably as she revisited memories of warm and loving times she and her daughter had together.

Gloria was Catholic, but the thought of Leticia being in heaven brought her no solace. She began to fear she was mentally unstable when friends, colleagues, and her husband continued to suggest that sufficient time had lapsed for her to let go of Leticia and move on with her life. I moved quickly to share with Gloria that there was no timetable on grieving and no right or wrong way to grieve, that the grief process was a very personal and individual experience and dependent upon many variables. I went on to say that feelings of grief complemented feelings of intimacy. In other words, grief is a manifestation of the loss of a loving and intimate relationship. I also went on to share that the depth of her pain represented the depth of her love for her daughter. I continued by letting her know that the grief process was not about letting go and moving on but was rather about accepting and embracing the loss of our loved one and then carrying them in a warm, endearing, and peaceful manner.

First I suggested that she create a sacred and spiritual place in her home that would include an altar table on which she would put a favorite picture of Leticia, what she considered to be sacred symbols of her faith, a candle, and her daughter's favorite flowers. Then I suggested that she establish a daily practice in which she would sit or kneel in prayer, meditation, and reflection before her altar. I explained the idea behind my suggestion was to formalize and ritualize her grief process and provide a quiet and safe place in which she could be alone to pray for and be with her daughter's spirit in the company of the Divine Presence, who would provide her warmth and comfort while she agonized over her loss. Finally, I shared with her the fact that meditation and reflection could be a healing experience, fostering symbolic repair, psychological and spiritual healing, emotional integration, and spiritual transformation. Participating in this process at my Ignatian Retreats had provided me with the gift of these insights, and I was hoping it would provide the same for Gloria. Thanks be to God, she eventually found the solitude she sought and with it, a more intimate relationship with God.

Healing

By the time I entered my first 30-Day Ignatian Retreat, I had laid to rest the major conflicts and issues that had plagued me throughout the years. I had overcome the shame that my mother had implanted in my spirit, made peace with her, realized and embraced the fact that I wasn't stupid and incompetent, completely removed the invisible barrier that I had constructed between me and Rosie, and put to rest the question of whether or not God loved me unconditionally. I still lacked the understanding that I needed healing from those experiences. This healing only came about with the soothing balm of God's infinite love, understanding, and compassion in which I was immersed throughout the retreat.

I learned from that retreat that the healing allowed me to rest in hope. This insight led me to recognize that clinical practice might not only help clients resolve the problems and issues they bring to therapy, but in many instances help them to heal from various psychological, emotional, and spiritual wounds caused by any number of traumatic experiences.

There is no greater recognition of this insight than is illustrated in a case presented in the professional journal *Social Work* by Ignacio Aguilar, a social worker at the Metropolitan State Hospital for the chronically mentally ill. In the article Ignacio describes how he works within a Mexican cultural context by speaking Spanish, creating a sense of community by working with clients as though they were members of a village, and taking into consideration customs and cultural styles in the decorations, furnishings, and program activities in his office. He also describes the use of ritual drama as a means of intervening. Such an approach is a dramatic enactment of a solemn ritual. In the case presented, it is an enactment of a funeral of a young girl's father. During the ceremony a table is used to represent a casket, members of the community are used as pallbearers, an individual is selected to represent the deceased, and Ignacio, bearing the mantle of a faith healer, is the ritual leader.

Ignacio and his colleague, Virginia N. Wood, write:

One 14-year-old girl had been having hallucinations in which her father appeared to her and told her she was "bad." This girl not only had unresolved feelings of grief and anger at the loss of her father, but also, after the father's death, had developed strong feelings against her mother. She resented the changes that had taken place, especially the family's move from Mexico to the United States, which resulted in her undergoing the physical and emotional changes of adolescence in strange surroundings. During the *velorio*, she slapped her father's face saying, "You were bad. You drank. You left us alone." Later she forgave him and asked his forgiveness, closed the coffin, and said, "*Descanse en paz* (Rest in peace)." She has had no further hallucinations of her father.[1]

On the surface it might be erroneously assumed that in his role as faith healer it was Ignacio and the ritual he performed that led to the young girl's recovery and spiritual transformation. But in fact, he was only an intermediary. It was the Holy Spirit working through him and the compassionate, understanding, and culturally sensitive atmosphere which he created and in which the girl was immersed that led to her healing.

> We all have the capacity to provide a safe, loving, accepting, and hopeful atmosphere in which spiritual healing can take place. We all have the capacity to allow the Divine Presence to work miracles through us.

My Catholicism has taught me that we are all children of God. The Divine Presence rests in all our souls. We have within us the capacity to heal from all the forms of emotional and spiritual suffering we experience. In our capacity as clinical practitioners, we can be a conduit for such healing.

We all have the capacity to provide a safe, loving, accepting, and hopeful atmosphere in which spiritual healing can take place. We all have the capacity to allow the Divine Presence to work miracles through us.

Another Wonderful Discovery

I believe that searching for how God works in our life provides the opportunity for endless discoveries regarding the varying dimensions of ourselves. Most recently, after reading Marcus Buckingham and Donald Clifton's book, *Now, Discover Your Strengths*, I discovered why I have excelled as a clinician. The premise of the book is that research has shown that individuals can only excel professionally if their "natural talents and strengths" coincide with the attitudes, gifts, and abilities required in achieving expertise and excellence in the occupation in which they have chosen to participate. To illustrate their point, they used Tiger Woods, Bill Gates, and Cole Porter as examples. In so doing, they described the natural inclinations and skills that allowed these three men to achieve superior levels of success.

Upon reflection I recognized that in addition to my personality and life experiences, I have been blessed with the natural talents and strengths required of an outstanding clinician, particularly the five principles I described above as being requirements of a spiritually based practitioner. Throughout my career, even as a novice, I had unknowingly been using, emphasizing, and relying upon these gifts. Sal, in acknowledging he couldn't teach me anything more, and Reverend Hoe, who perceived me as being wise, were the first to recognize these qualities. Even with their recognition, these talents remained beyond my conscious awareness, waiting to be discovered. Thanks be to God that through the circumstances that influenced my professional development the Holy Spirit has guided and provided me with mentors, opportunities, and experiences that eventually led me to recognize and embrace these hidden qualities.

A Journey of Love

My journey into spiritually based practice has been akin to my personal spiritual journey, taking me on unforeseen paths and trips while shaping and informing me in ways I could never have imagined. My career in clinical practice was founded on a medical model. With the evolution of the field came many changes, among them new models of therapy and a shift in attitude. Included in these changes was a shift from diagnosis to assessment, from psychopathology to presenting problems, from focusing upon deficits to focusing upon assets, from focusing upon illness to focusing upon wellness, from reliance upon theory to assist our clients to reliance upon evidence based on research, from looking at our clients from a very narrow perspective to looking at them holistically, and from "doing for" our clients to working "collaboratively with" them. I not only adapted to these changes, but in the process and, to my surprise, evolved into an expert practitioner, trainer, supervisor, and teacher. Even more surprisingly, I found myself contributing to my field by having professional articles and books published and developing my own distinct model for spiritually based therapy, with its emphasis on attending to the interior needs of clients with compassion, maintaining a healing frame of mind, and providing loving kindness, and hope.

As my career and professional development in clinical practice evolved, so did the love for my work. Words cannot adequately describe the satisfaction I experience in being present to the resolution of issues my clients bring to therapy, the joy I feel when I witness the transformation of their lives from chaos to peace, and the sense of wonder I encounter when I observe the healing of emotional wounds related to abuses, betrayals, and traumas that have plagued them for years. I cannot express the delight that bursts forth within me when I celebrate with them the good news that they will not die from the medical concerns they are facing. And I cannot tell you the fulfillment and affirmation I experience in assisting clients in reconciling their marital discord and reclaiming the peaceful and loving relationship they had lost, or helping them extricate themselves from an addiction that had for years consumed and in some instances, destroyed their lives. My work has led me to believe that one of the greatest honors I can receive is having individuals in the midst of pain, suffering, and confusion come seeking my assistance and guidance, inviting me into their stories and sharing with me their deepest fears, concerns, and vulnerabilities.

As much as I was enjoying my vocation, I was to receive even more blessings. As usual, without my knowledge or understanding at the time, The Holy Spirit would call me into even more precious work. My evolution into a spiritually based practitioner was preparing me to become a caretaker of souls. I was to become a spiritual director.

Chapter 9
Caring for Souls

> You have to be brave to follow God's tracks
>   into the unknown
> Where so many new things overwhelm
>   and panic you.
>
> HAFIZ

 The Holy Spirit surely works in mysterious ways. Much of my spiritual journey has been lived in the darkness of fear, guilt, ignorance, rigidity, doubt, confusion, and hopelessness. My faith led me to put up an invisible wall between me and Rosie, nearly destroying our love and our marriage. Yet, after years of languishing in the prison of spiritual depression and despair, I was sent a spiritual guide and mentor, Father Michael, who nourished my soul with his care, kindness, and wisdom. He provided me with the guidance I so dearly needed. I could never have imagined that I would someday be following in his footsteps. And yet, that is exactly what I was eventually called to do. As they did to Fatima in the fable recounted above, the tragedies and challenges in my life were preparing me for my ultimate vocation.

Like my psychological, professional, and spiritual growth, my journey into becoming a spiritual director has been an evolutionary, developmental, and adaptive process. Before being called to this holy art, I learned to lead retreats. In addition to planting the seeds for me to become a spiritually based practitioner, my experience was also preparing me to become a spiritual director. Like so many other things that happened to me during the course of my life, this added dimension to my career came as a complete surprise and under the most unexpected circumstances.

Creating a Context for Spiritual Work

Since we married so young and spent most of our young adulthood raising children, putting me through school, and developing my career, Rosie and I made a promise to ourselves that when we fulfilled our obligation of putting our children through college we would quit our jobs and fulfill our dream of taking a year off and traveling the world. So in 1990, when Eileen graduated from the University of California at Riverside and was settled in a job with the World Health Organization in Geneva, Switzerland, we began fulfilling that dream. I closed my practice, Rosie quit her job, and we set out on our journey. We began our travels by taking in the wonder and beauty of British Columbia and Alaska. We then headed to Switzerland to use Eileen's apartment as a home base to travel throughout Europe. It is there in December when I received a call from my sister Liz, telling me that our dad had had a stroke and was in a coma. Rosie and I flew home to be with him and help manage his care during his last days.

It was both a sad and enriching time. A few days following my father's death, Rosie's mom fainted and had to be hospitalized. We feared the worst. She remained in a stupor until diagnosed with a serious aneurysm that her physicians were able to effectively treat. Following these incidents with our parents, Rosie and I were emotionally drained. Becky, a friend of ours, recommended that we rest and recuperate by spending a quiet month in Lake Arrowhead. We took her advice.

It was a lovely and peaceful time. Rosie and I enjoyed the solitude—reading, playing games, resting by the fireplace, and taking walks in the surrounding neighborhood. During one of our walks we were immediately attracted to a striking two-story home that was up for sale. Among its attributes were large picture windows and spacious decks that allowed its inhabitants to enjoy the lovely surrounding landscape. Peeking through the windows we could see that the home was beautifully decorated with lovely paintings, furniture, and carpets. Suddenly, out of the blue, the idea of buying the place to provide professional training, personal enrichment, and marital retreats popped into my mind. The retreats would be non-religious and directed at anyone, religiously affiliated or not, interested in individual growth and development or improving and enhancing their marriage. I also thought I could use the facility to open an office and expand my private practice. To my surprise Rosie was in total agreement, adding that we could use the small inheritance I received from my dad as a down payment for its purchase. We were soon disappointed to learn that the house had already been sold, but were later blessed to build a beautiful home close by and adjacent to the San Bernardino National Forest where our retreatants could immerse themselves in nature.

A Place for Growth and Healing

Shortly before our first retreat I had a dream of our home being blessed by St. Joseph and the Virgin Mary. From that experience I felt our place was a sanctuary, a safe, warm, and loving environment in which people could come to rest, learn, and grow. I don't believe that it was a coincidence that our home wasn't ruined during the 2007 forest fire that destroyed many homes right in our neighborhood. I believe our sanctuary was protected by the blessing it received earlier so that Rosie and I could continue the work to which we were entrusted.

> I felt our place was a sanctuary, a safe, warm, and loving environment in which people could come to rest, learn, and grow.

Although the building of our Lake Arrowhead home was originally planned to cultivate personal and marital enrichment, to my surprise it also became a place for healing, reconciliation, and transformation. Many individuals came with the hope of finding peace and healing from wounds inflicted upon them in the past, wounds caused by, for example, being abused and neglected as a child, sexually assaulted, or involved in a violent relationship. Others came hoping to find reconciliation in their marriages or with parents with whom they had a strained, if not hostile, relationship. Still others, like Kathleen, who felt her narcissistic mother robbed her of both her innocence and identity, came hoping to find themselves. I was pleasantly surprised to find myself guiding retreats for small organizations in our home.

In addition to having participants complete inventories to examine different dimensions of themselves—like their degree of self-esteem, type of temperament, forms of intelligence they possessed, and their level of sensitivity—I used a self-devised set of ideas and experiential exercises to assist them in accessing and exploring their inner landscape. I also utilized many of the principles I observed during my Ignatian Retreats. These included the use of active imagination, creating ample time for stillness and reflection, and engaging participants in a process of reflection and discernment. There was for example, Ambrose, who was trying to decide whether or not to seek a divorce; Jessica, who was debating whether or not to change employment; and Rob, who was figuring out whether or not—because he had just been fired—there was something wrong with him.

Healing Old Wounds

Many retreatants attend my weekend retreats seeking a way to heal the resentful and painful feelings they hold towards their parents as well as the psychological insecurities they internalized as a consequence of a painful upbringing. One of my favorite exercises in helping them to discover the peace they are seeking is the use of creative-reflective writing. Research has shown that such writing can be a healing, transforming, and integrative experience, giving form to devastation, bringing order to trauma, and providing a means for recognizing and embracing one's interior goodness. With this in mind, I suggest to those suffering from the effects of having been abused, neglected, or treated with indifference by their parents to write a series of six letters to their parents that they will never send. For many, the letters are intended to help retreatants grieve the absence of a loving childhood, heal the emotional wounds inflicted upon them, remove negative self-perceptions and feelings of being worthless and unlovable, find peace with their parents, and grow out of the adversity in which they were immersed. To achieve their intended purpose, the letters were to be written to each parent individually and not to be edited. They were to express and reflect whatever thoughts, feelings, and images that came to mind at the moment.

The first letter has the writer imagine that if they had an enriching family life what their hopes and dreams might have been. Dreams, as I share with retreatants later, are a means by which we can be in touch with our interior goodness, because they originate from our souls and are an expression of our spiritual innocence. Dreams are also gifts to ourselves that say we wish to participate in all the goodness this world has to offer. In addition, they are a manifestation of our creative spirit and speak to the inner awareness that—given our gifts and talents—all things are possible. Finally, dreams can bring us warmth, joy, and peace, even before they are realized. By describing the manifestation of a beautiful family, retreatants describe and affirm undiscovered dimensions of themselves. For example, Edward, who suffered from an extreme negative image, wrote that he dreamed that he and his mother could have had a warm, loving, and caring relationship. After he shared this with me, I suggested that those attributes of an enriching relationship that he just described were an expression of his interior goodness—otherwise he couldn't have desired such a connection. Edward was able to comprehend and embrace my observations. This first letter also allows writers like Edward to be in touch with feelings associated with the absence of a loving, enriching, and happy childhood. As painful as it may be, this process allows people to heal from their emotional wounds, freeing them to move on in a meaningful, enriching, and hopeful manner.

The second letter asks participants to describe what they lost because of their miserable childhood, the third what their parents lost, and the fourth what they all lost. After giving thought to what they had written, retreatants are asked to write a fifth letter describing what they have learned about themselves, relationships, and the world in general. This letter is intended to assist them in gaining greater self-awareness while providing a path upon which they can move forward. Finally, the sixth letter is intended to help them grow from their pain and suffering and offers them hope for an enriching future. With this in mind, they are asked to describe their current dreams (and, if they don't have any, to use their imagination to discover them) and how their new insights might be used to achieve those dreams.

Another favorite exercise was suggested to me by my friend Diane Schuster. Retreatants are asked to draw their history as far back as they can remember to the present. They are to use symbols to represent special and significant moments or turning points in their lives and color to describe the mood during periods in their journey. They are also to mark the time when they felt they turned into an adult. There are no specific objectives for this exercise, other than helping people get in touch with their interior landscape. They are asked to enter the exercise with no particular expectations and to let the experience reveal to them whatever is necessary.

With the exercise I am always amazed at how creative and artistic participants can be. I am also amazed at the discoveries many of them make. Joanna, for example, discovered how strong and courageous she had been in encountering and overcoming numerous challenges throughout her life, among them coping with the death of her beloved father at the age of twelve, being diagnosed with ovarian cancer, and being abandoned by her husband and left with the responsibility of raising their two adolescent children. Then there was Priscilla who, after drawing a dark cloud over the day of her wedding, discovered that she never loved her husband, Phillip, and only married him out of the fear of being single. Dissatisfied with the marriage, she blamed him for their unhappiness when in fact she was responsible for their situation. With her new discovery she decided to share with Phillip what she had learned and in the process apologize and ask for his forgiveness. In addition, knowing they could never be happy, she would also ask him for a divorce.

Little did I realize that my experience running retreats was preparing me to become a spiritual director. I often found myself not only attending to the psychological, interpersonal, and emotional needs of those attending the retreats, but to their spiritual needs as well. This was especially true when I encouraged them in exploring their interior landscape or assisted them in the process of healing.

Becoming a Spiritual Director

Margaret Guenther entitled her book on spiritual direction *Holy Listening: The Art of Spiritual Direction*. I certainly have found this to be true. Spiritual direction is an art, and at its heart is listening to people with a loving and holy presence. My foundation for being a spiritual guide was laid by Father Michael, who demonstrated to me this sacred practice. Although there was certainly more to learn, learning that could only come from experience and formal training, I felt that through my experience with him, coupled with what I had learned from my spiritual transformation, participation in my first 30-Day Ignatian Retreat, and my evolution into becoming a spiritually based practitioner, that the Holy Spirit had prepared me for this holy undertaking.

Although there are psychological benefits from it, spiritual direction is not therapy. This confusion may be attributed, in part, to some of the similarities between them. Like therapy, spiritual direction is a collaborative and cooperative process; both require trust and respect between those involved. And, like therapists, spiritual directors must be compassionate, prudent, and engage those they are serving with wisdom and loving kindness. This is where the resemblance ends.

The reasons individuals seek therapy are entirely different from the reasons they seek spiritual direction. The former are looking for help to resolve problems or issues that impede them from having happy and fulfilling lives. The latter are on a journey of discovery regarding their attitudes, values, beliefs, relationships, and faith. In the process they are seeking a loving union with the Divine Presence and, through that, peace with others and with all creation. Therapy is time-limited and ceases when a client's issues have been resolved. Spiritual direction, on the other hand, is timeless. Directees are on a life-long journey into faith, hope, and love with no shortcuts, no quick paths, and no hidden secrets. While on this journey they are continually working towards cultivating a spiritually enriching way of living. Finally, unlike therapy, spiritual direction is not a problem-solving process but rather a transformational one. This transformational process is one in which we are guided into living more fully in our true or authentic selves and led into discovering the Divine Presence that dwells within us.

Those seeking spiritual growth are embarking on a difficult journey. Quoting Ron Rolheiser, it is a journey requiring "that somehow we have to lose ourselves to find ourselves, die to come to life, and give so as to receive." This undertaking requires courage and hope because we are required to surrender ourselves to a journey into mystery and as Hafiz writes in the poem quoted at the beginning of this chapter, "You have to be brave to follow God's tracks into the unknown." I would add that upon entering this journey we don't have any idea regarding what challenges we may be required to face or what sacrifices we may be asked to make. Anchored in faith, we can only hope that we will find the wisdom, strength, and support to meet those challenges and make those sacrifices.

Living in consolation—that is in peace, enjoyment, and good health—or living in desolation—that is in despair, suffering, and poor health—can both provide the fertile soil from which spiritual richness can evolve and blossom. Spiritual progress requires discipline, prudence, temperance, fortitude, and a continuous effort to live in compassion and wisdom. A spiritually enriching life is lived in the ordinary and not the extraordinary, in solitude and not excitement, in decency and not self-indulgence; in short, it is a life lived in blessed simplicity.

> A spiritually-enriching life is lived in the ordinary and not the extraordinary, in solitude and not excitement, in decency and not self-indulgence.

Those involved in spiritual direction take a very active and responsible role in their directees' spiritual formation, one that requires caring for the mind, body, emotions and, of course, spirit. Contributing to their own care, directees, among other things, are encouraged to cultivate warm and nurturing relationships, attend retreats, eat well, exercise, read spiritual literature, journal, and most importantly, spend part of each day in reflection, meditation, or prayer. Some will go so far as to practice fasting and abstaining from taking meals. If they belong to a religious tradition, they will actively participate in it. Finally, directees take the responsibility for preparing for a regular meeting with their spiritual director—normally once a month.

Clinical practice is founded on a medical paradigm, with its emphasis on words and phrases like *pathology, deficits, weaknesses, fixing, curing, attachment, co-dependency, borderline per-*

sonality, addiction, weak ego, psychopathology, midlife crisis, inner child, and many others. The focus and language used in spiritual direction is quite different. The emphasis here is on *spiritual nourishment, living in the fruits of the spirit, and affirming our directees' spiritual growth and development.* Instead of using psychological vocabulary, spiritual directors use spiritual concepts and metaphors such as grace, authenticity, enlightenment, mindfulness, contemplation, wisdom of the heart, purity of spirit, and joyful living.

Probably the most significant difference between therapy and spiritual direction is in the differing responsibilities of a therapist and a spiritual director. As a therapist, I assist and intervene in helping clients find answers to the questions they bring to treatment. Father Michael once told me that "people turn to the Bible for answers, when in reality the bible raises questions." These questions allow people to ponder and discern their relationship to God and how God intends them to live their lives. As a spiritual director, I don't have and don't give answers to those I am directing, but instead I raise questions. These questions, which can be disturbing and very challenging, are aimed at helping my directees to discern their own truth, what lies in their own hearts, or what might be impeding their own spiritual growth. For Ray, for example, after admitting to himself that he was gay, what meaning did that realization have regarding his relationship with God? For Josefina, it was how the animosity she felt towards her mother-in-law could become her friend and part of her spiritual transformation. And for Regina, who was searching for a spiritual path, what was her definition of a spiritually enriching life?

As a therapist, I play a significant role in orchestrating the direction of the therapy of my clients. This is not the case in spiritual direction. Instead, I believe the Divine Presence is always in the room, orchestrating and providing the actual assistance. I first learned this from Father Bob Fabian, director of the 30-Day Ignatian Retreat I first attended, when he shared with us during the course of a meeting that the Holy Spirit was actually doing the guiding. The major responsibility of our directors was to stay out of the Spirit's way.

Besides recognizing that the Holy Spirit was in the room with us, I took two other things away from Father Fabian's instruction. First is the belief that when spiritual directees enter my office it is transformed into a holy sanctuary in which they can feel immersed in a loving, affirming, and nurturing refuge. To commemorate this sacred transformation, when I open my office for spiritual direction I light a candle and say a short prayer asking the Holy Spirit for guidance. And second, I surmised that in my role as spiritual director I must be quiet so that I can listen, be still so that I am fully present, and be empty so that the Holy Spirit can, using my gifts and talents, work and speak through me.

The Journey Begins

I received my first request for spiritual direction from a former therapy client in the spring of 1996. I felt truly honored and grateful that Jane would entrust me with guiding her on her spiritual journey. Contributing to my feelings of honor and gratitude was the fact that she herself was a seasoned and well-respected retreat leader and spiritual director. As so often happened throughout my life, people witnessed and acknowledged gifts and talents in me of which I was never aware. Never in a million years would I have thought I possessed the capacity for being a spiritual guide and caretaker of souls. I also would have never imagined being a vehicle the Holy Spirit would use to assist those seeking to cultivate a more enriching spiritual life and loving relationship with God.

In subsequent years, others representing various ethnic groups began to seek my guidance. Many have been referred to me by word of mouth; others have come because I am on the Diocese of San Bernardino's list of spiritual directors. While most are Catholics, those seeking my guidance also represent a range of Christian denominations and other faith traditions. Even though they have a common goal—to cultivate a more enriching spiritual life and a more intimate relationship with the Divine Presence—individuals come to me with different needs and questions, are facing different challenges, and are in different places spiritually.

There was Stephanie, who throughout the years I saw her lived in consolation. She was a contemplative with her daily life with her young children and husband, being totally devoted to praising and serving God. She and her family were blessed with good health, she was a leader and very active in various ministries in her church, and her husband had a successful and enriching career. She prayed daily, lived in the fruits of the spirit, and was filled with gratitude for the blessings that had been bestowed upon her. She came to see me for accountability, which was to have some assurance that she remained attuned to God's presence and direction. Throughout most of our sessions I simply listened and praised her for her love and devotion to God, and the care and service she provided in his name

Then there was Martha, a devout Catholic, who for years lived in spiritual desolation, feeling alienated from God's presence, questioning the sincerity of her spirituality, and agonizing over whether or not she was psychologically impaired or being tempted by the presence of evil. During those years with me she was faced with many challenges that tempted her to step off the agonizing spiritual path she was called to travel. In many of our sessions she would be emotionally spent, feeling helpless, hopeless, and at times abandoned. Yet during this period her journal writings revealed wonderful spiritual wisdom and insights regarding faith, hope, love, and devotion to God—revelations that I have encouraged her to publish. I could clearly see how the Holy Spirit was using her agony as part of her spiritual formation, and yet I also knew no words from me would provide her with any peace or consolation. The only things I could offer her were a compassionate presence and the assurance for which she was seeking that she was psychologically sound and the challenges she was facing were spiritual in nature. Other than that, I trusted in the Holy Spirit to care for her and provide the strength she needed to sustain herself in the midst of her anguish. Through God's grace, Martha was eventually pulled out of her emotional chaos and spiritual darkness into the light of wisdom and affirmation.

Peggy, a devout Catholic, lived for nearly a year in physical desolation, suffering from a serious spinal injury that caused her excruciating pain, pain that made it impossible for her to sit or sleep comfortably. Even though she eventually received medication that gave her some relief, she continued to live with a great deal of physical discomfort. And yet, rather than succumbing to feeling and believing that she was a victim, she offered her suffering up to God. She also sought to find meaning in her physical pain—meaning that could be used in helping her cultivate a more spiritually enriching life. In addition to seeking assistance in removing impediments to her spiritual progression, she turned to me for support and guidance in this area as well.

Christopher, for a variety of reasons, had lost faith in any organized religion. He believed that the church in which he was raised was rigid, controlling, insensitive, punitive, and irrational. Contributing to his skepticism was the hypocrisy of his parents, professing to be "good Christians" but living a life to the contrary. Despite his distaste for the religion in which he was raised, Christopher could not divorce himself from his feeling that there was something he needed that was missing from the spiritual lessons he had been taught as a child. He sought my assistance in helping him reconcile these mixed feelings and, in the process, to discover a framework upon which he could create a new spiritual path for himself. Chief among my responses was suggesting readings that I thought would be useful in helping him with his search. I also assisted him in getting in touch with his inner wisdom and defining what he believed to be a spiritual life.

The primary concern for Douglas, a recent directee of mine, was in discerning whether or not he was being called to enter religious life. Discernment, according to Pierre Wolff, "is the process of making choices that correspond as closely as possible to objective reality, that are as free as possible from our inner compulsions, and that are closely attuned to the convictions of our faith (or to our values system, if we have no religious belief)." This process also involves making a judgment, that is, using our intelligence to examine as openly and honestly all the facts that are necessary for someone to determine whether or not he or she should pursue a course of action. In the case of Douglas, that judgment was about becoming a priest or not. In pursuing what he believed might be his vocation, he was in search of his meaning in life and how he was going to be of service to, involved with, and enriched by his connection to his fellow human beings, creation, and God. With so much at stake, seeking consultation and guidance from a spiritual director was both wise and prudent. With Douglas, I acted as a sounding board and on occasion suggested information and experiences that I believed would contribute to his body of knowledge and understanding, raise important questions related to the issues that were involved, and challenge some premises upon which he was making his judgment.

In most instances, those seeking my guidance were on a clear path needing only an objective person to witness and confirm what they were doing and to point out obstacles that they might unknowingly be putting in the way of their spiritual progress. Rebecca, for example, lived in generosity, sincerity, and loving kindness, but sadly was overly scrupulous. To help alleviate this unnecessary burden, one that deprived her from living fully in her interior goodness, I suggested that she read Ernest Kurtz and Katherine Ketcham's informative and thought-provoking book, *The Spirituality of Imperfection*. Then there was Jonathon, who was cultivating patience, particularly with his wife, with whom he had a stressful relationship. In one of our sessions he alluded to how patient he was being with her. I responded by asking how that made him feel. He replied by saying that it was making his life much easier. I then asked if he was being patient for his own benefit or for hers. He recognized immediately that his patience was self-serving, something about which he was previously unaware. The major reason why we need the assistance of a spiritual director is because, like Jonathon, we all have blind spots that can impede our spiritual progress or worse, take us down a path of spiritual and moral decay.

Soul Friends

Towards the end of one of our sessions, Claire, who I had been seeing for some time, told me that "I knew her and that our souls had touched." I was first taken aback by her comments but upon reflection recognized that she was right. Later, after reading John O'Donohue's beautiful book on *anam cara*, the Celtic word for soul friend, I understood why Claire's words rang true. When you have traveled on a spiritual journey for an extensive period of time with someone who has entrusted you with the well-being of their spirit by sharing with you without any pretension or egotism their deepest and often most vulnerable thoughts and feelings, their moments of untold joy and indescribable despair, their regrets, guilt and shame, their devotion to their loved ones and God, then almost by definition you have been connected with them at the soul level. On this level you have become soul friends who are joined together in an intimate, enriching, and mutually transforming process. Although on one level I am being used by the Holy Spirit to guide those seeking spiritual direction, on another the Holy Spirit is using them to nourish and transform *my* soul.

> On one level I am being used by the Holy Spirit to guide those seeking spiritual direction. On another the Holy Spirit is using them to nourish and transform *my* soul.

Claire touched and enriched my spirit by demonstrating to me, even in the midst of her darkest despair, her commitment, devotion, and compassion to those women she was helping to overcome the negative and often traumatic effects of sexually assault. I was continually amazed by Stephanie's heartfelt praise of God for all the wonderful gifts that were bestowed upon her. I was moved and enriched by Martha's demonstration of faith, hope, and love while she traveled through the dark night of the spirit. Peggy enriched my soul by her blessed physical martyrdom, her totally selfless act of offering her pain and suffering up to God. And finally, there is Jennifer, who I haven't mentioned previously. She touches me at the deepest level of my being and has enriched my spirit throughout the years by her love and devotion to her family, her efforts to discard her egocentricity, her seeking of truth, her simple living, and finally by the manner in which she goes about cultivating a beautiful spiritual environment in which she can continue to grow in love, compassion, and generosity.

Because of their sanctity, these soul friends have strengthened and added depth to my faith, hope, and love in humanity and God in ways I could not have imagined. They have modeled for me what it means to live in purity of spirit and blessed simplicity. They have also demonstrated the meaning of living in prudence, justice, temperance, and fortitude. Needless to say, being a spiritual director has been a gift and a beautiful experience for me. It has been wonderful to see how the Divine Presence works in helping all of us—through consolation, desolation, and in the course of our everyday experiences—to live spiritually enriching lives regardless of any defining characteristics we might have or our adherence to any particular faith tradition.

A Final Blessing

The final significant occurrence that helped to solidify my evolution from therapist to spiritual director was the validation I received in 2010 at the Hesychia School for Spiritual Direction in Tucson, Arizona. I had experienced a significant increase in the number of people seeking spiritual direction from me, even though I had no formal training in this area. My knowledge and skill was derived from my clinical practice, readings on the subject, my experience of giving retreats, and from the spiritual direction that I had been receiving myself. Of course, my major resource came from being led and directed by the Holy Spirit. Although feeling competent in my new vocation, I still felt obliged to those that entrusted me with their spiritual growth to receive additional training. The opportunity to fulfill this obligation did not come about accidently.

At the suggestion of my own spiritual director at the time,

Father Cassian Lewinski, I decided to take a week-long silent retreat at the Desert House of Prayer in Tucson. Across from the retreat house was the Redemptorist Retreat Center that offered retreats and educational programs to those seeking spiritual growth. While walking out of their Our Lady of the Desert chapel after attending Mass, I caught a glimpse of brochures publicizing their program for training spiritual directors. I knew immediately that I was being called to attend that instruction. The curriculum was especially attractive because it was ecumenically based, integrating knowledge of spiritually from all the major forms of spiritual traditions including Judaism, Hinduism, Buddhism, and Native American spirituality.

I entered the program as though it were a retreat, with no preparation and no expectations. I entered it with the attitude of allowing the experience to unfold and with the belief that the Holy Spirit would be directing my journey, that I would take away what God wished me to know, acquire, or experience. Because I opened myself up to whatever was to come, it turned out to be an amazing spiritual experience.

The program consisted of lectures on various dimensions of spiritual direction, presentations by speakers representing different faith traditions, and a practicum in which we were supervised in both the giving and receiving of spiritual direction. There was no new information regarding various faith traditions presented, but there was definitely a deep appreciation of them all. Most impressive and inspiring were the presenters themselves. I was drawn into the obvious beauty of their spirituality. Regardless of their religious orientation, they were obviously very spiritual human beings, exuding sincerity, warmth, kindness, devotion to their faith, and a compassionate presence. I especially appreciated the experiential dimensions of their presentations, which were heartfelt, engaging and enriching, giving me a glimpse of what it might feel like to be immersed in their faith tradition. Victoria Redhawk Steele, for example, invited us to participate in the Native American peace pipe ceremony. What I took away the most from them was their collective warmth and deep sense of connection with the Divine Presence, which in turn helped me to further recognize and appreciate the fact that spirituality has no boundaries and that there are many paths to developing a spiritually enriching life.

I returned from Tucson filled with gratitude for the experience. Not only were the program and presenters wonderful, but so were my fellow participants. They, like the instructors, represented many faith traditions and a variety of roles within them. Like everyone associated with the program, they were also deeply spiritual. I felt safe enough to expose myself and be directed by them in our practicums, experiences that turned out to be surprisingly enriching and enhanced my spiritual formation. In describing my Hesychia experience to a friend, I said with deepest sincerity that I felt "bathed in love." My Hesychia experience has made me feel more secure and confident as a spiritual director while offering me even greater hope that I can be an instrument of the Holy Spirit in helping those seeking intimacy with God.

Epilogue

 I'm writing these afterthoughts sitting in the Skywalker room at the top of the Golden Princess cruise ship. As I relax, admiring the lovely panoramic view of the Pacific Ocean before me, I am reminded of how God continues to bless me with a beautiful life. Rosie and I were blessed a few days ago when we visited another of God's Cathedrals, the Iguazu Falls in Argentina. Like our first visit to the Grand Canyon on our honeymoon, this majestic, spectacular, and sacred landscape filled us with joy while taking our breath away. We are blessed with excellent health, even after having turned seventy a few months ago. Our children and grandchildren continue to do well, and in a few months we will be celebrating our 50th wedding anniversary. We are also blessed with a loving family, dear friends, and much to which we look forward. My love for and relationship with God continues to grow. Upon reflection, the words of Erwin McManus I mentioned earlier, "God calls us out of the life we have known and calls us to a life we have never imagined," resonates even more deeply. As I alluded to throughout this narrative, in my childhood and young adult life I would have never anticipated the life that I now enjoy.

Upon reflection it is plainly evident that the Holy Spirit has been accompanying and guiding me throughout my journey. It is now evident to me that particular teachers, mentors, and spiritual directors were put in my path as guides to provide me the care and support I so desperately needed. It is now evident that I was being called by God to enter the field of social work and within this profession to serve the needs of others in the roles of educator, clinical practitioner, and now spiritual director. It is now evident that I was guided into developing a spiritually based practice, the touchstones of which are faith, hope, and love. It is also clear how *all* my life experiences and natural talents prepared me for my vocation. The three realms of my life, those being my psychological, professional, and spiritual, were weaved together in a manner that allowed me to discover my authenticity.

It is obvious to me that God has invited me into a loving and intimate relationship with him. I did nothing to deserve all the blessings I have received; they were simply gifts from a benevolent, compassionate, and loving God. Finally, I now know that I was called to share with you my story so that you might acquire a greater understanding of the psychology and the spirituality of hope.

In conclusion, I wish to share that shortly before my 70th birthday I closed my clinical practice in Colton, the city adjacent to my home in Riverside. My decision for its closing was based primarily on another unforeseen event, the purchase of their dream home in the city of Pasadena by my daughter, Eileen, and her husband, David. As a result of their plan to remain in Hong Kong until David's retirement, they asked Rosie and me to move in and see to the Pasadena home's care. It was easy for us to acquiesce to their request because we love the attractive landscape in which their home is located as well as the intellectual, cultural, and entertaining opportunities the surrounding community has to offer. It remains to be seen whether or not I will reopen a clinical practice nearby. In the meantime, I continue to provide spiritual direction, conduct clinical workshops, and offer retreats in Lake Arrowhead. I also rest in the hope that the Holy Spirit will again, in these later years of my life, reveal yet once again what God intends for me.

Notes

Introduction
1. *The Poems of Emily Dickinson*, edited by Thomas H. Johnson, Cambridge, Mass.: The Belknap Press of Harvard University Press, Copyright ©1951, 1955, 1979, 1983 by the President and Fellows of Harvard College
2. McManus, E.R. (2006). *Soul Cravings*. Nashville, Tennessee, Thomas Nelson, Destiny, entry 9.
3. Pieper, J. (1986). *On Hope*. San Francisco: Ignatius Press, p. 26. Chapter 2

Chapter 3
1. McManus, E.R. (2006). *Soul Cravings*. Nashville, Tennessee: Thomas Nelson, Destiny, entry 7.

Chapter 6
1. Tagore, R. (Translated from Bengali to English by the poet) "Stray Birds," #150, 1916, MacMillan.

Chapter 7
1. Kidd, S. M. (1990). *When the Heart Waits: Spiritual Direction for Life's Sacred Questions*. San Francisco: Harper and Row, p. 5.

Chapter 8
1. Aguilar, I. and Wood, V. N. (1976). *Therapy Through a Death Ritual*. Social Work 21(1). 53.

References

Buckingham, M., and Clifton, D. O. (2001). *Now, Discover Your Strengths*. New York: The Free Press.

DeSalvo, L. (1999). *Writing as a Way of Healing*. Boston: Beacon Press.

Guenther, M. (1992). *Holy Listening: The Art of Spiritual Direction*. New York: Rowman & Littlefield Publishers, Inc.

Housden, R. (2003). *Ten Poems to Open Your Heart*. New York: Harmony Books.

Keating, T. (1994). *Intimacy with God*. New York: The Crossroad Publishing Company.

Kurtz, E., and Ketchman, K. (1993). *The Spirituality of Imperfection: Storytelling and the Search for Meaning*. New York: Bantam Books.

Nouwen, H. J. M. (2004) *Out of Solitude: Three Meditations on the Christian Life*. Notre Dame, Indiana: Ave Maria Press.

Merton, T. (2002). *No Man Is an Island*. New York: Harcourt Inc.

O'Donohue, J. (1997). *Anam Cara: A Book of Celtic Wisdom*. New York: Cliff Street.

O'Donohue, J. (2004). *Beauty: The Invisible Embrace*. New York: Harper/Collins Publishers.

Shah, I. (1967). *Tales of the Dervishes*. New York: E. E. Hutton.

Steindl-Rast, D. (1984). *Gratefulness, the Heart of Prayer*. New York: Paulist Press.

Acknowledgments

I am indebted to my dear friend Diane Schuster without whose support, consultation, and editing throughout the years this book could not have been written.

Furthermore I wish to thank my friends Elizabeth Brenenstall, Barbara Cox, Victoria Delesandro, Carolyn Havert, Maria Martinez, Greg and Lili Moore, Lorrie Rosner, and Pat Tanner for reading my manuscript and providing me with valuable comments. I also wish to thank Mike Coyne and Greg Pierce for their fine editing and helping me bring my message to you with greater clarity.